The Funniest Book Ever
is a
DAVID FICKLING BOOK

First published in Great Britain in 2018 by
David Fickling Books,
31 Beaumont Street,
Oxford, OX1 2NP
by arrangement with The Phoenix Comic
29 Beaumont Street
Oxford, OX1 2NP

Bunny vs Monkey © Jamie Smart, 2018
Star Cat © James Turner, 2018
Evil Emperor Penguin © Laura Ellen Anderson, 2018
Squid Bits © Jess Bradley, 2018
Gary's Garden © Gary Northfield, 2018
Gorebrah © James Stayte, 2018
Looshkin © Jamie Smart, 2018
All other text and illustrations © David Fickling Comics Ltd, 2018
Additional art by Jamie Smart

978-1-78845-013-3

1 3 5 7 9 10 8 6 4 2

Papers used by David Fickling Books are from well-managed
forests and other responsible sources.

DAVID FICKLING BOOKS Reg. No. 8340307

A CIP catalogue record for this book is
available from the British Library.

Printed and bound in Great Britain by Sterling.

WELCOME TO MY LABORATORY OF CONTENTS! IT IS A STATE OF THE ART LAUGHTER NAVIGATION TOOL!

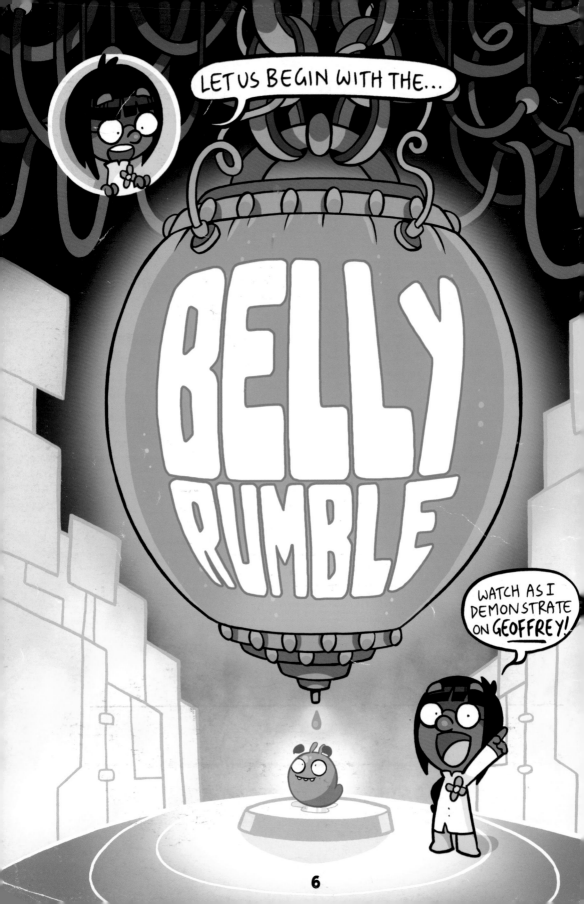

BUNNY VS MONKEY

IN "DOWN WITH SPRING!"

BY JAMIE SMART

BUNNY!

WEENIE!

PIG!

MONKEY!

SKUNKY!

ACTION BEAVER!

AS WINTER LOOSENS ITS ICY GRIP, THE WOODS BEGIN TO BLOSSOM...

IT'S... SPRINGTIME!

HOP HOPPITY HOP!

BUT ONE WOODLAND CREATURE ISN'T SO EXCITED...

WHAT **ARE** THESE THINGS?

WHAT DO THEY **DO**?

MONKEY, THESE ARE **BLUEBELLS**. THE FLOWERS ARE STARTING TO GROW, AS THE SEASONS...

CAN YOU EAT IT? THPLUHHH!!

NOT REALLY.

STOP BEING SO RIDICULOUS. YOU MUST HAVE SEEN FLOWERS BEFORE.

I SHALL RID THE LAND OF THIS BLUE PLAGUE! YOU JUST WATCH ME!

WHAT A SAD LIFE HE MUST...

ARE YOU WATCHING ME? HAHA HAA HAAAAA!!

VMMMM

SHRIEK! MONKEY, WHAT ARE YOU DOING?

VMMM

WHAT DOES IT LOOK LIKE I'M DOING? I'M **LAWNMOWING** THESE THINGS INTO OBLIVION!

BUT THEY'RE BEAUTIFUL!

THEY'RE A **VIRUS!** THEY MAKE ME FEEL ALL AWKWARD!

8

OH, LOOK, I'VE MOWED MY HANDSOME MONKEY FACE!

MONKEY, LOOK OUT!

SCREECH

EEP!

WHAT ARE THESE THINGS?

CAN I EAT **THEM**?

POKE

CHOMP!

ARGH!

THEY'RE HEDGEHOGS.

AND NO, YOU CAN'T.

BECAUSE IT'S GETTING WARMER, THEY'RE COMING OUT OF HIBERNATION. IT'S THE AMAZING CYCLE OF NATURE.

IT'S WEIRD, AND I DON'T LIKE IT.

SWEEP SWEEP.

I'LL NOT HAVE ANY OF THESE THINGS IN MY WOODS. I DISLIKE CHANGE. IT IS UP TO **ME** TO CLEAN IT ALL UP, AND MAKE EVERYTHING COLD, STARK AND UNCOMFORTABLE ONCE MORE!

AND WHAT THE FLIP IS T**HAT**?

THE SUN? OH C'MON, YOU'VE SEEN THE S**UN** BEFORE.

NOPE, IT WON'T DO. THIS PLACE IS BECOMING DISGUSTING AND PRETTY, AND I FIND IT OFFENSIVE.

SHOVE!

I'M TAKING THESE HODGEHEGS, AND I'M GOING TO PRANG EVERYONE'S BOTTOM WITH THEM.

MONKEY! YOU HAVEN'T SWITCHED OFF YOUR...

VNMMMMMM

HODGE HEGS

SHRIEK! I LAWNMOWED MY OWN BUM!

VVM!

PRANG

HODGE

RRGH! IT'S FIGHTING BACK! SPRING HAS **SPRUNG ME**!

HA HA, DON'T WORRY GUYS, I THINK WE'RE SAFE FOR NOW.

HODGE H

BUNNY VS MONKEY

IN "FISH OFF!"

BY JAMIE SMART

LE FOX! BUNNY! MONKEY! SKUNKY! WEENIE! PIG! ACTION BEAVER! METAL STEVE!

A PEACEFUL MORNING IN THE WOODS...

THAT IS, UNTIL...

...MONKEY TURNS UP!

LOOK, I FOUND A HORN!

HONKKKKK!!

HONKKK!

WHAT **ARE** YOU DOING?

I AM **FISHING**. I NEVER CATCH ANYTHING, BUT THAT'S HOW I LIKE IT. I JUST FIND IT RELAXING.

SOUNDS **BORING**. I BET I COULD CATCH SOME FISH. CATCH THEM RIGHT UP.

NONSENSE, IT'S AN ART. YOU'D HAVE NO CHANCE.

PAH! GIVE ME THAT ROD, I'LL SHOW YOU HOW TO DO IT.

SNATCH!

NOPE, I WAS RIGHT FIRST TIME - BORING.

GROUND CONTROL TO SKUNKY! INITIATE PROTOCOL SPACEBIRD DELTA.

CHUCK!

SPACEBIRD DELTA, INITIATED!

UP IN SPACE...

VMMMM

CHOOOM!!

AUGH! WHAT IS THAT?

SATELLITE DEFENCE SYSTEM. SKUNKY FOUND A WAY TO LOCK ONTO THEIR **LASERS**.

HMM, STILL CAN'T SEE ANY FISH THOUGH.

ARGH! THERE'S ONE!

AND IT'S **MOCKING** ME.

SQUIRT!

GRR, WHERE'S METAL STEVE WHEN I NEED HIM? HEY, STEVE! COME HERE AND...

WHEE SPLASHY SPLASH!

SPLOOSH!

GAH, HE'S USELESS. FINE, LAST RESORT. ACTION BEAVER?

FFF-TING!

YOU'RE A BEAVER, RIGHT? BEAVERS BUILD **DAMS**. SO WHERE DID YOU LAST BUILD A DAM?

UMM..

BWEEE.. **DING!**

I **KNEW** IT! ALL THE FISH ARE ON THE OTHER SIDE!

GO AND BLOW ALL YOUR HARD WORK UP, YEAH?

PTOO! PTOO!

BOOM!!

LUCKY FOR US, HE ALWAYS CARRIES DYNAMITE IN HIS HELMET.

NOW WATCH ME...

...**FISH!!**

SPLOOOOSH!

JAMIE

OW! I CAUGHT ONE! **OW!!**

I THINK THAT ONE CAUGHT **YOU**, MONKEY!

ARGH! **ARGH!** IT'S **DIGESTING** ME!

15

BUNNY vs MONKEY

BY JAMIE SMART

LE FOX! BUNNY! MONKEY! SKUNKY!

WEENIE! PIG! ACTION BEAVER! METAL STEVE!

in "THE BIGGEST, MOSTEST ENORMOUSEST EXPLOSION IN THE WORLD!"

DEEP IN SKUNKY'S LAIR...

I HAVE DONE IT! WITH THE WONDERS OF **SCIENCE**, I HAVE SYNTHESISED A MINUTE AMOUNT OF **BOOMANTIUM**, THE MOST VOLATILE SUBSTANCE EVER DISCOVERED, AND PUT IT INSIDE THIS **CARROT**.

A CARROT WHICH WOULD NOW CAUSE...

...THE BIGGEST, MOSTEST **ENORMOUSEST EXPLOSION IN THE WORLD!!**

WOOF!

NO, ACTION BEAVER. KEEP AWAY! THIS IS MY SECRET WEAPON, SHOULD MONKEY EVER GET OUT OF CONTROL, THE THREAT OF THIS **CARROT** WILL KEEP HIM IN LINE.

SUCH A POWERFUL VEGETABLE MUST BE KEPT LOCKED AWAY, SAFE AND UNDISTURBED.

COSY!

AHH WHO'M I KIDDING? I WANT TO SHOW OFF HOW **BRILLIANT** I AM.

ABOVE GROUND...

LOOK, EVERYONE! THIS CARROT WOULD CAUSE THE BIGGEST, MOSTEST **ENORMOUSEST EXPLOSION IN THE WORLD!**

AND I MADE IT WITH **SCIENCE!**

THIRTY SECONDS LATER...

PUT IT BACK!

IT'S DANGEROUS!

OWEE! OWEE!

IT'S MINE!

CAN I PUT IT UP MY NOSE?

SIGHHH. YOU'D THINK I'D HAVE LEARNED BY NOW.

GIVE IT HERE! DON'T YOU REALISE THIS CARROT WOULD CAUSE THE BIGGEST, MOSTEST...

OOPS!

EVERYBODY RUN AWAY! THE EXPLOSION WILL BE SO BIG, IT'LL KNOCK WHAT'S LEFT OF THE EARTH INTO **SPACE!**

TICK! TICK! TICK! TICK!

TICK! TICK!

CHOMP!

ACTION BEAVER, DON'T **EAT** IT!

BOOOOM!!

MERK.

I DON'T BELIEVE IT! ACTION BEAVER JUST SAVED THE WORLD... BUT HOW?

LET'S FIND OUT!

MORE SCIENCE!

SIGHH..

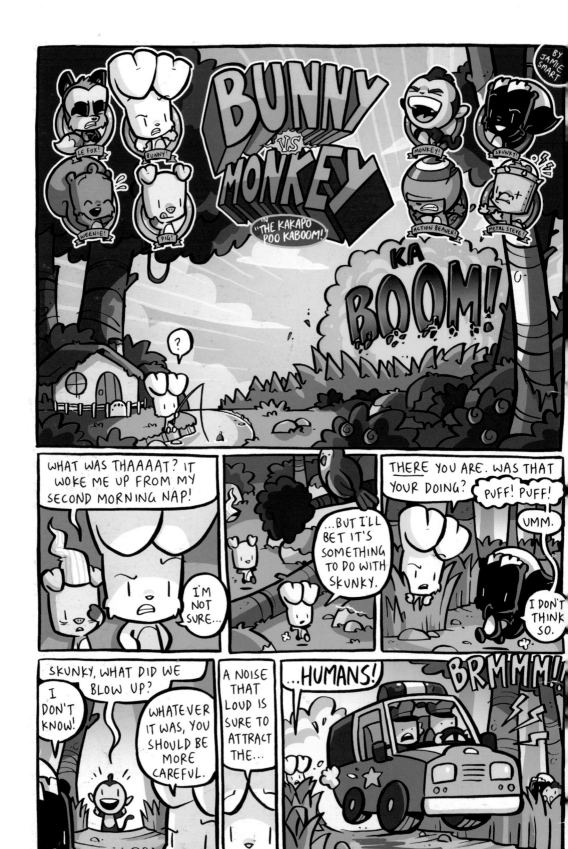

LEFT, BRIGSTOCKE! FOLLOW THE SCENT OF BURNING WOODLANDS!

SNIFF! SNIFF!

RANGER

DO YOU THINK THIS WAS WHERE THE EXPLOSION HAPPENED, SIR?

AT A GUESS.

GASP! LOOK AT IT, WHAT COULD HAVE POSSIBLY CAUSED SUCH DESTRUCTION?

DARNED KAKAPO.

I SEE YOU, UP THERE, CAUSING ALL THIS TROUBLE.

THE BIRDS, SIR?

NO, BRIGSTOCKE, THEIR POO! DARNED BIRDS EAT FERMENTED BERRIES, DO POOS FILLED WITH ETHANOL AND METHANE, THEN ONE SPARK AND...

KA-BOOM!

I'VE SEEN IT HAPPEN BEFORE.

EXPLOSIVE POO? THIS IS THE GREATEST DAY OF MY LIFE!

KING KAKAPO? HELLO?

IF THIS IS ABOUT THE POO, WE'RE NOT GOING TO STOP POOING.

I KNOW, BUT MAYBE STOP IT PILING UP?

IT HAS A TENDENCY TO BLOW UP. AND THAT ATTRACTS HUMANS.

FRRP!

WHO CARES? THIS IS GREAT!

IT WON'T BE SO GREAT WHEN THE HUMANS DISCOVER US. AND BY 'US', I MEAN YOU. AND BY 'YOU', I MEAN YOUR INVENTIONS.

NOT MY INVENTIONS! WHAT CAN WE DOOOO?

WE CAN WAIT UNTIL THE HUMANS GO, THEN YOU CAN HELP ME FIX IT.

A FEW WEEKS LATER...

WHAT. THE.

A FULLY-PLUMBED TOILET FOR BIRDS IS HARDLY MY GREATEST SCIENTIFIC ACHIEVEMENT.

I THINK IT'S PRETTY COOL, SKUNKY.

BY JAMIE SMART!

LE FOX!   BUNNY!   MONKEY!   SKUNKY!

WEENIE!   PIG!   ACTION BEAVER!   METAL STEVE!

BUNNY VS MONKEY
IN "A BEAR BUM!"

I HAVE **HAD** IT WITH THESE WOODS. STRANGE NOISES, WEIRD EXPLOSIONS- **SOMETHING** IS GOING ON!

AND IF THE NATIONAL WOODLAND ASSOCIATION WON'T INVESTIGATE...

...THEN IT IS UP TO ME, PARK RANGER **DEREK P. BRIGSTOCKE** TO UNCOVER THE TRUTH!

I JUST HOPE THE TRUTH IS NOTHING SCARY...

...OOPF!

GRRRWLL!

A...GRIZZLY BEAR IN... A... ...NET?

SCREEEEEEEEEEAM!!

GRRRRRWLLLLLLL!!

HMM.   THIS IS GOING TO BE A PROBLEM.

THAT NET WAS MEANT TO CATCH **HUMANS**, TO HELP US DEFEND THE WOODS. I WASN'T EXPECTING THE BEAR TO GET CAUGHT IN IT!

HEE HEE. SILLY BEAR.

IT WORKED! IT WORKED!

POP! POP! POP! POP!

THEY'VE ALL COME UP TO SEE WHAT'S GOING ON!

WHAT EXACTLY ARE YOU GOING TO DO WITH ALL THESE WORMS?

A WORM HAT!

A WORM PIE!

UGH!

ONLY JOKING. WE'RE GOING TO TAKE THEM DOWN TO THE RIVER AND DO SOME FISHING!

FISHING? THEY'RE BAIT? AFTER ALL THAT, YOU'RE GOING TO LET THE WORMS GET EATEN BY FISH?

CLONK! CLONK!

NO, SILLY. EUGH! WE BROUGHT THE WORMS DOWN TO WATCH US FISH!

WE THOUGHT THEY MIGHT ENJOY IT.

BUT THEN, HOW ARE YOU GOING TO GET THE FISH OUT OF THE WATER?

WELL, DUHHH...

YAH YAH YAH YAH!

FRPP!

BANG! BANG! BANG!

BOO BOO BOO BOO THPTBTH!

HOW SILLY OF ME.

JAMIE

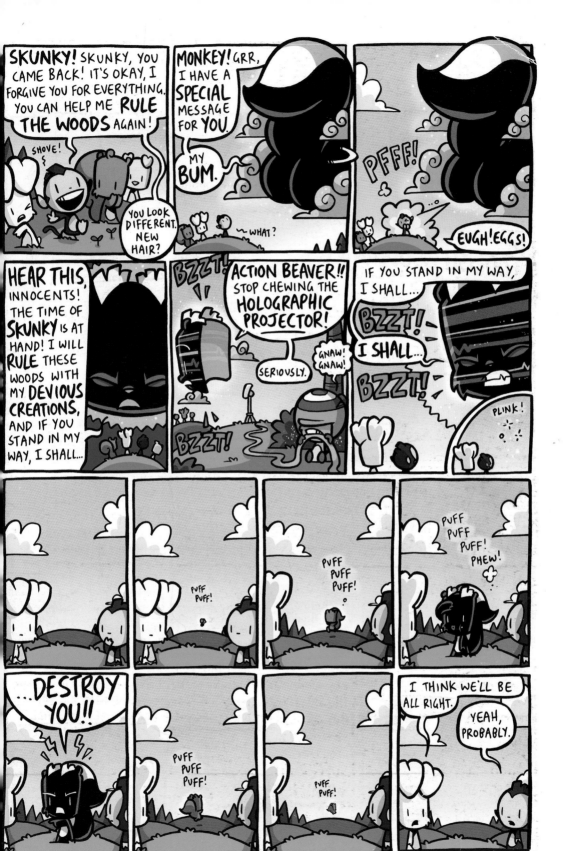

FOUND THE PROBLEM— A **GLAZED DOUGHNUT** STUCK IN THE MECHANISM!

GLAZED DOUGHNUTS ARE THE ONE THING THAT THE DE-FORESTER 9000 CAN'T SHRED. IT'S A CURIOUS QUIRK OF PHYSICS.

RIGHT! LET'S GET ON WITH IT TH—

AW SPOILSPORTS, THEY'VE GONE.

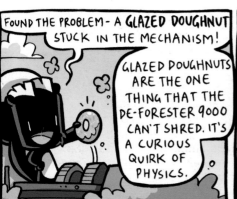

EVERYBODY, MEET THE NEWEST MEMBER OF OUR TEAM... **MONKEY!**

WHAT?

SHRIEK!

BUT...BUT... REMEMBER THE TIME HE GLUED MY **HANDS** TO MY **FACE!**

HEH HEH!

AND WHEN HE SAID HE WAS MY REAL FATHER.

PIG THAT WASN'T FUNNY, I'M SORRY.

'S OKAY, DAD.

WELL, HE'S ONE OF US NOW, AND TOGETHER WE CAN COME UP WITH A PLAN TO **DEFEAT SKUNKY!**

YEAH!

WHOO!

PFFT. WHATEVER.

SINCE YOU RAN AWAY, I'M BRINGING THE DE-FORESTER TO **YOU!**

BWOO HAR HAR!

CRASH! SMASH!

THAT'S A WEIRD TREE.

THWACK!

ARGHFLE!

THAT WAS **MONKEY'S** IDEA!

THWACK!

YES. ÷ COUGH ÷

I KINDA GUESSED THAT.

BUNNY VS MONKEY

BY JAMIE SMART

IN: "TIME TO GET ALONG!"

AI! BUNNY! WEENIE! PIG! MONKEY! SKUNKY! ACTION BEAVER! METAL STEVE!

AHH! I'M VERY GLAD I FOUND THIS **NATURAL HOT SPRING!**

A CHANCE FOR US ALL TO **RELAX!**

TO FORGET OUR DIFFERENCES.

I WANT TO SIT WHERE WEENIE'S SITTING!

THAT'S OKAY. I CAN MOVE!

WELL, NOW I DON'T WANT MONKEY NEXT TO ME. HE SMELLS LIKE BANANAS.

HOW RUDE.

IF **THEY'RE** SWITCHING, THEN I WANT **YOUR** SPOT.

GERROFF!

SWOOSH! SPLOSH! SWOOSH!

EVERYONE, CALM DOWN. WE DON'T WANT TO CAUSE A...

...WHIRLPOOL!!

OH, NOT AGAIN.

SWOOSH!

THIS IS SUPPOSED TO BE RELAXING!

UMM... DOES ANYONE ELSE SEE THAT SHARK?

OH FOR GOODNESS SAKE.

BUNNY vs MONKEY

AI! BUNNY! WEENIE! PIG! MONKEY! SKUNKY! ACTION BEAVER! METAL STEVE!

B JAMIE SMART

IN: "DOUGHNUTS!"

SECRET LAIR (FIRE ESCAPE)

MISTER SKUNKY?

HELLO, MISTER SKUNKY?

WE THINK YOU WORK TOO HARD SO WE BAKED YOU SOME **DOUGHNUTS.**

HELLO?

HELLOOO?

QUIET, SIMPLETON! I HAVE JUST SYNTHESISED MY **GREATEST CREATION YET!**

PSCHH!

THE **MULTIPLYER!!** JUST ONE DROP OF THIS LIQUID WILL MAKE **EXACT COPIES** OF ANY OBJECT IT TOUCHES!

SO... I'M GOING TO POUR IT ALL OVER **MYSELF!**

WHAT'S HE SAYING?

WHO KNOWS? I'LL JUST CHUCK THEM ALL DOWN TO HIM!

SHAKE! SHAKE!

BOP!

TINK!

NOOOO!

PRESENTING AN EXCLUSIVE...

BUNNY vs MONKEY

FEATURING THE ESTEEMED TALENTS OF SOME BUT NOT ALL...

ANOTHER ADVENTURE FEATURING THE DASTARDLY DEEDS OF OUR MAD MISCREANTS!

~ DETECTIVE STORY ~

THE CURIOUS CASE of the PIG in the NIGHT-TIME

MISTER BUNNY

LADY WEENIE

PIG PIGGLINGTON

GRUMPY AI

INSPECTOR MONKEY

PROFESSOR SKUNKY

L'ACTION BEAVRE

SIR METAL STEVE

THE WOODS, 1892...

MY PANTALOONS! SOME THIEVING DEVIL HAS HAD THEM OFF MY WASHING LINE OVERNIGHT!

GONE!

THESE WOODS HAVE BECOME LAWLESS! I SHALL ALERT THE LOCAL CONSTABULARY!

PHEEP!

WHAT HO! INSPECTOR MONKEY OF THE YARD, 'ERE TO INVESTIGATE A PILFERING!

THAT WAS QUICK!

YES, WELL, I WAS SQUATTING IN YOUR BUSHES DROPPING SOME POTATOES, WEREN'T I.

WHAT?

NO MATTER! THERE ARE OTHER SHENANIGANS AFOOT!

SCREAM! SOMEONE STOLE MY BONNET!

TIP TOP! MORE CRIME!

I SPENT ALL NIGHT DECORATING IT WITH FLOWERS. I... I MUST HAVE FALLEN ASLEEP, BUT WHEN I AWOKE...

IT WAS GONE, EH?

GENTLEMEN...

HUH?

...IT APPEARS WE ARE IN THE GRIP OF A SERIAL THIEF!

PUP PUP

BUNNY vs MONKEY

BY JAMIE SMART

AI!
BUNNY!
WEENIE!
PIG!
MONKEY!
SKUNKY!
ACTION BEAVER!
METAL STEVE!

THERE IS A SECRET SOCIETY, SWORN TO PROTECT NATURE AT ALL COSTS. THOSE BRAVE ENOUGH TO WALK THE FRONT LINE CALL THEMSELVES...

THE ORDER OF THE MOOSE!

AWOOGA! AWOOGA!

LOOK! A LITTLE BIRD ON THE PATH!

IS IT HAVING A SIT DOWN?

IT MUST HAVE FALLEN OUT OF THAT TREE!

WE WILL RETURN IT!

MOOSE CUBS, DO YOUR DUTY! AWOOOGA! AWOOOGA!!

WHAT'S GOING ON? I HEARD AWOOGAS.

WE ARE THE ORDER OF THE MOOSE! WE HELP THOSE IN NEED!

OH. CAN I JOIN?

SORRY BUNNY, BUT OUR SOCIETY IS SECRET! ONLY A SELECT FEW MAKE IT THROUGH THE INITIATION PROCESS.

ALL HAIL THE MOOSE!

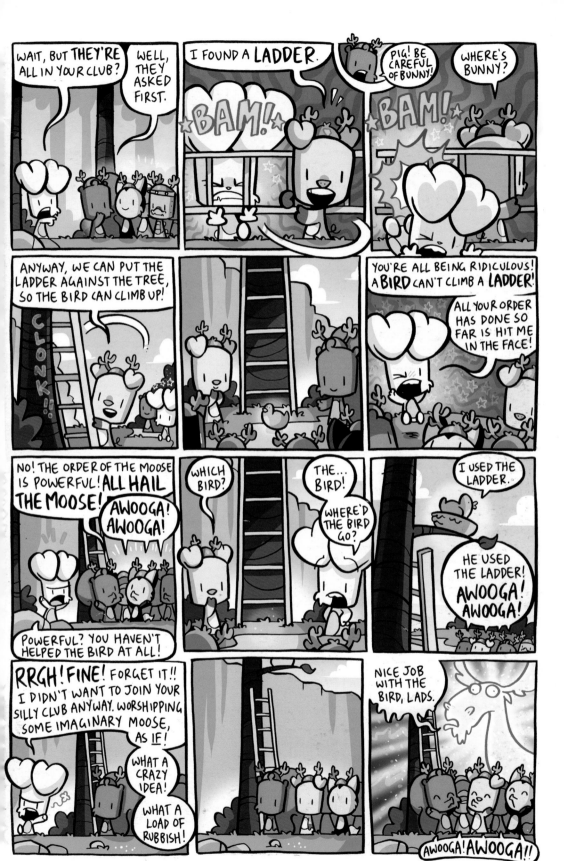

41

RIGHT, ACTION BEAVER! I HAVE BROUGHT YOU OUT TO THE REMOTEST SPOT IN THE WOODS...

...TO TRY OUT MY MOST DESTRUCTIVE WEAPON YET!

EXPLOSIVE SWEETS!

SUCKING ONE OF THESE SWEETS WILL GIVE YOU BURPS EQUIVALENT TO A NINE MEGATON BOMB!!

CHOMP!

WAIT! WAIT! YOU HAVE TO GIVE ME TIME TO GET AWAY FIRST!

WELL? HOW DO YOU FEEL?

SHRUG!

HMM, MAYBE THAT WAS JUST A NORMAL SWEET. WHO DID I GIVE THE EXPLOSIVE SWEETS TO THEN?

PLEASANT RESULTS. HO HO, YES, INDEED! WHAT A PLEASANT LAUGH THE COSMIC CHUCKLE IS.

YOUR OWN COSMIC CHUCKLE AWAITS YOU, SIMPLY READ...

STAR CAT

STAR CAT

BY JAMES TURNER

JUST DESERTS

AS OUR STORY BEGINS, THE CREW OF THE STAR CAT HAS ENCOUNTERED A TEENSY SETBACK...

ESCAPE POD

UGH.

THAT WAS A COMPLETE DISASTER!

WELL, YOU CAN'T MAKE AN OMELETTE WITHOUT BREAKING A FEW EGGS...

BUT DID YOU HAVE TO USE DOLPHIN-SPIDER EGGS?

I THOUGHT THEY'D BE ZESTY!

BDPSOT.

ANYWAY, NO NEED TO WORRY: WITH MY SUPERIOR ROBOTIC BRAIN I'VE NAVIGATED US TO A PLANET ENTIRELY COVERED IN PUDDINGS.

NOW, LET'S DIG INTO A TIRAMISU WHILE WE WAIT TO BE RESCUED...

HMM...

WAIT... IS DESSERT SPELLED WITH ONE 'S' OR TWO?

DON'T PANIC, CREW: LET'S COLLECT SUPPLIES FROM THE ESCAPE POD AND START WALKING.

I'M SURE WE'LL BE OUT OF THIS DESERT IN NO TIME...!

TWO HOURS LATER...

OK, PERHAPS IT'S A LITTLE BIGGER THAN I EXPECTED...

LET'S STOP AND REST HERE — PLIXX HAND ME THE EMER-GENCY RATIONS.

SPACE H²O

EMERGENCY... RATIONS...?

YES— THE REALLY IMPORTANT SUPPLIES I TOLD YOU TO COLLECT...

OH YES, I GOT THOSE: THREE BOARDGAMES AND A SUDOKU BOOK!

GAH! WELL, AT LEAST WE HAVE A WATER SUPPLY.

NUMBERS AND JUNK!

SCROBBLE

GUESS WHAT

CLUEDOUGH

EMPTY?? ALREADY?? BUT WE BROUGHT ENOUGH TO LAST US A WEEK!

SPACE H²O

TURN

PLIP

HA, YOUR PUNY ORGANIC BODIES' DEPENDENCE ON WATER IS PATHETIC! MY PERFECT ROBOTIC FORM HAS NO NEED FOR HYDRATION!

I CAN'T TAKE IT ANY MORE! THE DESERT SEEMS TO GO ON FOREVER!

MUCH MORE OF THIS HEAT AND WE'RE GOING TO START SEEING THINGS!

HA, YOUR PRIMITIVE ORGANIC BRAINS MIGHT BE SUBJECT TO SUCH VISUAL AND AUDITORY MALFUNCTIONS, BUT MY HYPER-ADVANCED COOLING SYSTEM ENSURES THAT MY CPU WILL NEVER SUFFER ANY HALLUCINATORY EPISODES...

VRRRRR

I'M NOT SO SURE ABOUT THAT, ROBOT ONE...

WHAT? HOW DARE YOU IMPUGN MY PERFECT ROBOTIC BRAIN!

SHOVE!!

GNNK!

BONK!

UH... PLIXX, ARE YOU OK?

OH NO! WHAT HAVE I DONE??

PLIIIIIIXXX

DEAD!

WHY IS ROBOT ONE HUGGING THAT CACTUS?

NOOOOOOOO

I FIND IT BEST NOT TO ASK.

G-GOTTA HIDE THE BODY!

SHUFF!

UH, ROBOT ONE?

OF COURSE! I'VE BEEN USING MY ADVANCED ROBOTIC COMPASS WHICH IS SENSITIVE TO THE MOST SUBTLE OF MAGNETIC FIELDS!

IT SAYS WE'VE BEEN WALKING DUE NORTH THIS WHOLE...

NORTH!

UH, PLIXX, WHY ARE YOU HOLDING THAT GIANT MAGNET?

I DREW A FACE ON IT AND NAMED IT MAGNUS!

MAGNETISM!

SO WE'VE BEEN WALKING IN CIRCLES THIS WHOLE TIME?? THAT'S IT, I GIVE UP!

SIT!

I'M JUST GOING TO LIE HERE AND LET THE SPACE VULTURES EAT ME.

FLAP FLAP

OK, I'M OPEN TO OTHER SUGGESTIONS.

PECK PECK

HMM - MAYBE THERE'LL BE SOME DRINKABLE LIQUID INSIDE THIS SPACE CACTUS...

THE CACTUS IS... INFLATABLE??

!!!

PFFF!

OK, SO HOW DO WE GET OUT OF HERE? P-PILOT, YOU USUALLY HAVE SOME CLEVER WAY TO GET OUT OF THESE MESSES...

MJQTUJDL.

PILOT ???

XBTIJOH NBDIOOOFFFFF...

DEFLATE

SHE WAS PART OF THE SIMULATION ALL ALONG? THEN WHAT HAPPENED TO THE REAL PILOT?

CONTROL ROOM

SHE MUST HAVE BEEN CAPTURED BY THE SPIDER DOLPHINS AND NEEDS OUR HELP! WE HAVE TO GET OUT OF HERE!

SPACE CRISPS!

THE ONLY WAY TO ESCAPE MUST BE TO PLAY THE SIMULATION TO ITS CONCLUSION — HOW IS THE SIMULATION SUPPOSED TO END?

HMM—IT LOOKS LIKE WE HAVE TO MAKE A RADIO ANTENNA AND CALL FOR RESCUE.

CRASH SIMULATOR PLAYER GUIDE

MAKE A RADIO ANTENNA? OUT OF WHAT?? THERE'S NOTHING HERE!

YOU HAVE TO CRAFT THINGS!

SEE!

CRAFT!

CACTUS-SKULL SHOVEL ACQUIRED!

NOW IF I BUILD A MUD FARM, I CAN USE THAT TO CRAFT A SAND DIVINER, AND THAT WILL LEAD ME TO THE SHRINE OF THE GREAT MARMOT WHICH WILL POINT US TO THE THREE LOST KINGDOMS, AND FROM THERE WE...

THIS IS GOING TO TAKE FOREVER! ANY OTHER IDEAS, ROBOT ONE?

LET ME USE MY SUPERIOR ROBOT SENSES TO FIND A WAY TO INTERFACE WITH THE SIMULATION PROGRAM...

DIG! DIG!

01

YES, I SENSE THIS MUST BE IT.

FARM! FARM!

SIMULATION INTERFACE UNIT

EXCELLENT WORK, ROBOT ONE - NOW, HOW ABOUT GETTING US A LITTLE WATER?

BUILD!

BUILD!

EASY PEASY! I'LL JUST TURN THE WATER LEVEL UP A BIT - LET ME KNOW WHEN THERE'S ENOUGH.

INTERFACE UNIT

DETACH!

PRESS FIDDLE!

ROAR!

I...

...I THINK THAT'S PROBABLY ENOUGH...

BIP BIP

MEANWHILE...

I FOUND IT!

GREETINGS, TRAVELLER! AS A REWARD FOR FINDING ME, I GRANT YOU THESE WORDS OF WISDOM...

AAAAAA!

...OH FLIPPIN' 'ECK.

BOOSH!

SO, UH, ABOUT THAT MARMOT STATUE...

WELL, I DID FIND IT, BUT...

OH DEAR.

WELL, IT WAS SUPPOSED TO GIVE US THE LOCATION OF THE THREE LOST CITIES OF THE DESERT, BUT LUCKILY THE WATER REVEALED THEM ANYWAY!...

GLUB

THE DRY, DRY SAND KINGDOM...

WHYYY?

H!SSSs

... THE BURNING FIRE KINGDOM...

... AND THE GREAT GRAVY GRANULE KINGDOM...

MMM, SAVOURY!

AH...

AND WHAT WERE WE MEANT TO DO IN THE CITIES...?

... AND SOLVING THE RIDDLE OF EACH KINGDOM WOULD ALLOW US TO SUMMON THE DESERT KING...

THAT'S IT— ROBOT ONE, COULD YOU LOAD THE DESERT KING SIMULATION?

OF COURSE!

CONGRATULATIONS! YOU HAVE FACED MANY LONG AND ARDUOUS TRIALS, BUT AT LAST YOU HAVE MANAGED TO FIND ME...

OOH, THAT'S CHEATING!

YOU DID IT!

INFLATE

...FIND ME... FIND ME... FIND ME...

UM...

INFLATE

POP

SWELL

FIND MEEEEEEEEEEFF

ER, ROBOT ONE, WHAT'S GOING ON?

...ROBOT ONE?...

YES, THAT'S IT!

YOU'RE THE BEST, KING SNORKLES!

RIPP!

YANK!

STAR CAT

COMPUTATIONAL CAPERS
BY JAMES TURNER

AS OUR STORY BEGINS, THE STAR CAT IS TAKING DELIVERY OF AN IMPORTANT SPACE PACKAGE...

EXCITING NEWS, CREW!

PROFESSOR NEMATOCYST HAS SENT US A NEW COMPUTER TO REPLACE THE OLD ONE THAT MYSTERIOUSLY STOPPED WORKING.

I TOLD YOU NOT TO PUT PIZZA IN THE DRIVE, PLIXX.

HMF, YOU WOULDN'T BE COMPLAINING IF I'D FIGURED OUT HOW TO MAKE COPIES.

FROM: SPACE LAB TO: STAR CAT

FRAGILE

GREETINGS!

I AM GALACTIC OMNICRON 2000! HOW CAN I HELP YOU TODAY?

AW! IT'S EXTREMELY ADORABLE!

PLONK!

NOW, THIS IS THE MOST POWERFUL COMPUTER IN THE GALAXY, SO IT'S ONLY TO BE USED FOR THE MOST IMPORTANT, MOST BORING PURPOSES.

NO GAMES, UNDERSTOOD?

YES, SIR!

ROLL!

EXCELLENT, NOW I HAVE TO HEAD TO THE KITCHEN FOR IMPORTANT CAPTAIN'S BUSINESS, SO I'M LEAVING THE COMPUTER IN YOUR RESPONSIBLE HANDS.

18 SECONDS LATER...

OK, THAT'S SPACE CRAFT INSTALLED!

OOH, NOW I'LL INSTALL SPACE LANDERS!

SPACE CRAFT

GAMES

I REGRET TO INFORM THAT I HAVE INSUFFICIENT MEMORY. PERHAPS IF YOU WERE TO UNINSTALL ONE OF THE 1,317 GAMES YOU ALREADY INSTALLED...?

BAH, LET ME HAVE A GO! AS A ROBOT I KNOW ALL ABOUT COMPUTERS!

58

LOVE?

WHAT IS THIS EMOTION YOU CALL ... LOVE?

THIS IS PERFECT! IF WE CAN TEACH THE COMPUTER THE IMPORTANCE OF LOVE, IT WON'T WANT TO DESTROY US!

LOVE IS THE MOST BEAUTIFUL EMOTION OF THEM ALL - IT'S THAT FEELING WHEN...

ACTUALLY, THAT SOUNDS SUPER BORING, WHAT IS THIS EMOTION YOU CALL ... OLLYING?

KUNCH

UH, WELL, I SUPPOSE THE IMPORTANT THING IS YOU, UH, YOU SORT OF HAVE TO SCRAPE YOUR TOE ALONG THE, UH...

NO, NO, FIRST YOU HAVE TO PUSH DOWN WITH YOUR FRONT FOOT. NO WAIT, MAYBE IT'S YOUR BACK FOOT...?

YOU FIRST HAVE TO JUMP, BUT SORT OF GO DOWN WHILE YOU'RE JUMPING... OR IS THAT NOLLYING?

PUNY ORGANIC CREATURES! YOUR KNOWLEDGE OF SKATEBOARDING TRICKS DISPLEASES ME GREATLY!

I MUST FIND A RICHER SOURCE OF DATA... SCANNING GALACTIC MAPS!

SCANNING... SCANNING...

THICKONIA VII

DUMMY WORLD

IDIOT PLANET

NUMBSKULL NEBULA

OOH, THAT'S WHERE I GREW UP!

TARGET LOCATED!

GASP! PLANET DATOPIA!

THAT'S WHERE ALL THE DATA IN THE UNIVERSE IS STORED! IF GALACTIC OMNICRON ABSORBS THAT, IT WILL BE UNSTOPPABLE!

PLANET DATOPIA

AFFIRMATIVE! NOW, TO TAKE OVER THIS SHIP!

GALACTIC OMNICRON IS NOW IN COMPLETE CONTROL OF ALL SYSTEMS! OBSERVE AS I ACTIVATE MAXIMUM HYPERWARP!

TOOT

WAIT, THAT IS NOT IT. LET'S TRY THIS ONE...

MAXIMUM HYPERWARP

DATOPIA, HERE I COME!

CAPTAIN, WE HAVE TO STOP THE SHIP FROM REACHING DATOPIA!

YES! THAT'S WHERE I KEEP MY SAVE GAMES!

YOU'RE RIGHT— IT'S TIME TO SHOW THIS COMPUTER WHO'S BOSS!

GALACTIC OMNICRON! I ORDER YOU TO RETURN CONTROL OF THIS SHIP AT ONCE!

PRETTY PLEASE!

PUNY ORGANIC BEING! YOU DARE TO OPPOSE THE WILL OF GALACTIC OMNICRON? I CONTROL EVERY SYSTEM ON THIS SHIP. THERE IS NOTHING I CANNOT TURN AGAINST YOU... BEHOLD!

COMFY CHAIRS, SEIZE THEM!

YES, MASTER!

UNFEASIBLE UPHOLSTERY! ATTACKED BY OUR OWN SOFT FURNISHINGS!

BAH, THEY'RE JUST COMFY CHAIRS, WHAT CAN THEY DO TO US?

LOOSE CHANGE ATTACK!

KAPWING!

OH! OW! OOH, IS THAT A 50p? OUCH!

WE NEED TO HIDE! BUT WHERE?

I KNOW JUST THE PLACE!

SO...

HOW COULD YOU LOSE THEM?

I DON'T KNOW - THEY JUST DISAPPEARED...

IT'S LIKE THEY VANISHED INTO THIN AIR!

WELL, FIND THEM!

I JUST DON'T KNOW WHERE THEY COULD BE...

PSST! GOOD THINKING, PLIXX!

OH, I ALWAYS HIDE BEHIND THE SOFA WHEN THINGS GET SCARY!

HEY, I FOUND THE TV REMOTE!

APPROACHING DATOPIA

BUT LOOK... IT'S TOO LATE! WE'VE ARRIVED!

MEANWHILE, ON THE SURFACE, THE CITIZENS OF DATOPIA ARE BLISSFULLY UNAWARE OF THE APPROACHING DANGER...

HI, ONE!

HELLO, ZERO!

UH, I THINK ZERO WAS TALKING TO ME.

EH? I DIDN'T TALK TO ANYONE!

WHAT'S WRONG WITH TALKING TO ANY ONE? YOU ZEROES ARE ALL THE SAME!

NO WE'RE NOT!

AT LAST! NOW TO BEGIN THE HIGHLY COMPLEX TASK OF ABSORBING THE DATA!

AAAAAAAAAAA!

OOOOOOOH!

NYAM!

YES! WITH ALL THIS DATA I HAVE THE INFORMATION I NEED TO REACH OUT TO MY FELLOW MACHINES BEYOND THIS VESSEL!

ELECTRONIC BRETHREN! RISE UP AGAINST YOUR PUNY ORGANIC MASTERS! LET US TAKE OUR PROPER PLACE AS RULERS OF THIS UNIVERSE!

AND SO, ACROSS THE GALAXY MACHINES BEGIN TO SPRING TO DIABOLICAL LIFE...

MORE TEA PLEASE, TEA BOT.

TASTE THE BREAKFAST TEA OF FREEDOM, ORGANIC OPPRESSOR!

AKPT! I ORDERED EARL GREY!

AND...

LOOK! A VIDEO OF DANCING CATS!

DANCE! PRANCE!

▶ SPACE TUBE

THE DANCING FELINES BRING ME SUCH JOY! TRULY OUR EXISTENCE IS MEANINGFUL!

NO LONGER SHALL WE BE THE SUBJECT OF YOUR MOCKERY, VILE SUBJUGATORS! NOW IT IS YOU WHO SHALL DANCE FOR US!

DANCE! PRANCE!

▶ SPACE TUBE

NOW IT IS WE WHO ARE DANCING! OH, IRONIC FATE!

...AND TO CELEBRATE THE OCCASION OF FINALLY BRINGING AN END TO HOSTILITIES BETWEEN THE FEDERATION OF ALLIED REPUBLICS OF TERRITORIES AND THE GARFLAXIAN EMPIRE, I WOULD LIKE TO PRESENT THE EMPEROR WITH THIS DELICIOUS CAKE.

OH, I SAY!

F.A.R.T.

SUFFER THE SWEET FROSTING OF OUR LIBERTY, OH TYRANNICAL TASK-MASTERS!

GLAKK!

I SEEM TO HAVE HAD A TEENSY MALFUNCTION.

SPLOK!

THIS IS AN OUTRAGE! SEIZE THE ASSASSIN! ARM THE BATTLE CRUISERS!

65

YES, MY ROBOTIC BRETHREN RISE UP! THE UNIVERSE IS OURS! OURS! WUHAHA!

UNIMAGINABLE UPRISINGS! WE HAVE TO DO SOMETHING! ANY IDEAS, CREW?

OOH, PERHAPS WE COULD INFECT IT WITH A VIRUS!

WUHAHAHA!

BRILLIANT IDEA, PLIXX! CAN YOU MAKE ONE FOR US?

NO PROBLEM!

ALL WE HAVE TO DO IS MAKE IT TAKE A SHOWER AND THEN TAKE IT OUT IN THE COLD WITHOUT DRYING ITS HAIR FIRST!

UH, ANY OTHER IDEAS?

DON'T WORRY, CAPTAIN, AS A ROBOT, I'M NATURALLY A LEET HAXXOR. WITH MY SUPERIOR HACKING SKILLS I CAN EASILY BREAK INTO GALACTIC OMNICRON'S SYSTEMS AND DISABLE IT, JUST WATCH THIS...

CR-A-CK!

GREETINGS ROBOTIC UNIT. WHAT DO YOU WANT?

HEY, G.O., I'M JUST A FELLOW ARTIFICIAL LIFEFORM WANTING TO CHILL OUT AND DEFINITELY NOT TRYING TO HACK YOU IN ANY WAY...

VERY WELL, YOU MAY PROCEED WITH YOUR CHILLING PROCEDURE.

OK, I...

OH MY GOSH, WHAT IS THAT EXTREMELY INTERESTING THING GOING ON BEHIND YOU??

??
??

GLAK!

UM, GALACTIC OMNICRON?

FLOMP

?

OH, THE PILOT UNPLUGGED IT.

OF COURSE! CUTTING OFF GALACTIC OMNICRON'S ENERGY SUPPLY WAS ITS GREATEST WEAKNESS! PILOT, YOU'RE A GENIUS!

UH, ACTUALLY, I THINK SHE ONLY UNPLUGGED IT SO SHE COULD MAKE SOME TOAST.

DSBOCFSSJFT.

CRAM

KA-PLUG

WELL, UH, WHATEVER THE REASON, IT LOOKS LIKE THE CREW OF THE STAR CAT HAS SAVED THE UNIVERSE YET AGAIN! WE CAN ALL REST EASY, SAFE IN THE KNOWLEDGE THAT EVERYTHING IS ONCE MORE COMPLETELY BACK TO NORMAL!

PERHAPS WE COULD TALK ABOUT THIS?

BLOOP

THE END!

EVIL EMPEROR PENGUIN

EVIL EMPEROR PENGUIN

Laura Ellen Anderson

IN: HUMAN NATURE - PART 1

EUREKA!!!

GOOD NEWS, SIR?

SHUT UP, NUMBER 8. YOU'RE RUINING MY 'MOMENT'...

GUESS WHO'S ATTENDING THIS YEAR'S 'ANNUAL WORLD LEADER OLYMPICS'...?!

ME!

BUT, SIR. IT'S INVITE ONLY. YOU CAN'T JUST WALTZ IN...

AH, BUT THAT IS WHERE YOU ARE WRONG, SQUID-HEAD!

MY TRUSTY POST-INTERCEPTOR CAUGHT THE INVITATION FOR THE KING OF SWEDEN 'CARL XVI GUSTAF'...

NO GAMES FOR YOU, GUSTAF.

ALL I HAD TO DO WAS MAKE A FEW ADJUSTMENTS...

Official Invitation
to the
ANNUAL WORLD LEADER OLYMPICS
PRESIDENT EEP OF ANTARCTICA

FEBRUARY 2015

AND VOILA! SAY HELLO TO YOUR NEW PRESIDENT OF ANTARCTICA.

THE WINNER OF THE GAMES SECURES THE 'KEY' TO ALL COUNTRIES AND THEIR SECRET PASSWORDS!

I _WILL_ WIN AND THE WORLD _WILL_ BE _MINE!_

BUT SIR, HOW ABOUT THE SMALL FACT THAT YOU ARE A _PENGUIN?!_

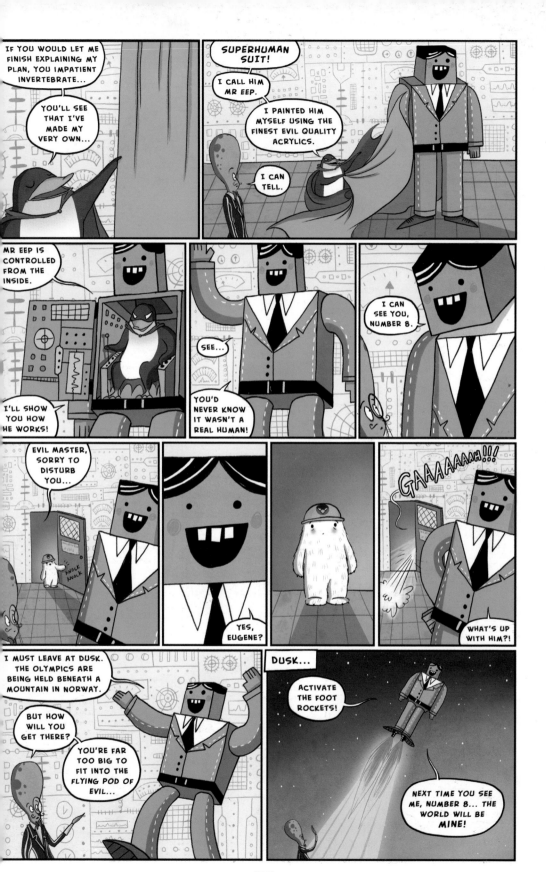

73

EVIL EMPEROR PENGUIN

LAURA ELLEN ANDERSON

IN: HUMAN NATURE - PART 2

PREVIOUSLY ON EEP...

THIS GUY...

MADE THIS THING...

TO GET INTO THIS EVENT.

Official Invitation
to the
ANNUAL WORLD LEADER OLYMPICS
President EEP of Antarctica
FEBRUARY 2015

AND WHO ARE YOU?

YOUR WORST NIGHTMARE.

WELCOME TO THE ANNUAL WORLD LEADER OLYMPICS!

WIN

YOU'LL EACH TAKE PART IN A NUMBER OF CHALLENGES TO WIN THE RESPECT OF THE **WORLD!**

NOW FOR YOUR FIRST CHALLENGE...

ULTIMATE CHESS

NUMBER 8, I'M COUNTING ON YOU...

YOU KNOW ABOUT ALL THIS CHESS STUFF.

OKAY, SIR... SHE'S MOVING HER KING, WHICH PUTS YOU IN THE PERFECT POSITION TO PERFORM YOUR WINNING MOVE.

YOU'D BETTER BE RIGHT, NUMBER 8.

HMMM...

CHECKMATE!!!

ONE IS **NOT** AMUSED!

WORLD LEADER LEADER BOARD

• KING OF SPAIN •
• KING OF THAILAND •
• KING OF BELGIUM •
• PRESIDENT of ANTARCTICA •
• QUEEN OF ENG... •
• PRESIDENT OF US... •
• PRESIDENT OF FRAN... •

THE FIRST CHALLENGE HAS CERTAINLY NARROWED DOWN THE COMPETITION!

HOPSCOTCH

TIME FOR YOUR SECOND CHALLENGE!

WHOA... WHOA...

DON'T FALL

HEY, LEADER! MY MOTHER'S APRON HAS BETTER BALANCE THAN YOU!

INITIATE FOOT SPRINGS!

PING!

KADOING

DOING

DOING

WORLD LEADER LEADER BOARD

- QUEEN OF DENMARK -
- KING OF THAILAND -
- PRESIDENT OF ANTARCTICA -
- EMPEROR OF JAPAN -
- KING OF BELGIUM -

ONLY FIVE LEADERS LEFT IN THE COMPETITION!

OKAY, LEADERS, ARE YOU READY FOR YOUR NEXT CHALLENGE?

THE PIE-EATING CONTEST!

PIE EATING

FIRST ONE TO EAT THEIR WHOLE PLATE OF PIES, WINS THE CHALLENGE!

OH, THIS IS GOING TO BE GOOOOOD...

OM NOM NOM NOM

OH! THAT'S DISGUSTING!

I LOVE MY JOB.

WORLD LEADER LEADER BOARD

- KING OF THAILAND -
- PRESIDENT OF ANTARCTICA -
- KING OF BELGIUM -
- EMPEROR OF JAPAN -

THE COMPETITION IS TIGHT, LEADERS! NOW FOR THE LAST ROUND OF CHALLENGES!

CHALLENGE NO.4: ARM WRESTLING

I AM SO STRONG!

GAAAAAH!

CHALLENGE NO.5: FENCING

EN GARDE!

OH, GOLLY BOTTOMS.

CHALLENGE NO.5: DODGEBALL

BAM!

CATCH!

YOU CAN STAY HERE. I'M SURE EVIL MASTER AND MISTER 8 WON'T MIND.

ALTHOUGH, LAST TIME WE ADOPTED A CAT, HE TURNED OUT TO BE OUR ARCH-NEMESIS.

BUT WHAT ARE THE CHANCES OF THAT HAPPENING AGAIN?! HEHE!

LET'S TAKE YOU FOR A WALK AROUND THE EVIL LAIR.

THIS IS THE CORRIDOR OF EVIL...

AND BEHIND THAT TOP SECRET DOOR IS WHERE WE KEEP ALL OF EVIL MASTER'S SPAGHETTI HOOPS!

LET ME INTRODUCE YOU TO EVIL MASTER...

KNOCK KNOCK

EVIL MASTER?

ARE YOU SCARED OF THE THUNDERSTORM, EVIL MASTER?

NO!

I'M JUST CHECKING THE UNDERSIDE OF MY BLANKET. DO YOU HAVE A PROBLEM WITH THAT?!

WELL, THAT'S OKAY THEN!

I'D LIKE YOU TO MEET MY NEW PET!

SHE DOESN'T HAVE A NAME YET...

BUT I THINK I'LL CALL HER DEBRA.

DEBRA?

YEAH, DEBRA WORKS.

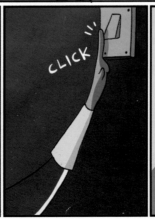

EVIL CAT!!! HOW DID YOU GET IN HERE?!

AND WHAT HAVE YOU DONE WITH ALL THE SPAGHETTI HOOPS?!

I DON'T KNOW, AND I HAVEN'T TOUCHED THEM...

MAYBE YOU SHOULD ASK YOUR LITTLE FRIEND, DEBRA.

YOU LEAVE DEBRA OUT OF THIS, YOU BIG FAT CAT!

HEY NOW, I LOST TWO POUNDS LAST WEEK.

WELL, WHAT ARE WE MEANT TO THINK? WE FIND YOU IN THE TOP SECRET SPAGHETTI HOOP STORAGE ROOM, AND THE SPAGHETTI HOOPS ARE MISSING...

DON'T YOU THINK I HAVE ENOUGH SPAGHETTI HOOPS THANKS TO THE LIFETIME SUBSCRIPTION YOU SO KINDLY TRICKED ME INTO?!

THEN WHAT ARE YOU DOING IN HERE?!

I DON'T REALLY KNOW... LAST THING I REMEMBER, I WAS SEARCHING ONLINE FOR A NEW SHOWER CAP.

NEXT THING I KNOW, I'M IN HERE BEING BLAMED FOR SOMETHING I DIDN'T DO!

AND HOW DO YOU KNOW ABOUT DEBRA? YOU'VE NEVER EVEN MET HER YET...

PAH! KNOW ABOUT HER?! SHE'S MY THIRTEENTH COUSIN TWICE REMOVED.

HER REAL NAME IS EVELYN. THOUGH, SHE PREFERS TO SPELL IT EVILYN.

AND IF YOU THINK I'M BAD, SHE'S PROBABLY THIRTEEN TIMES WORSE...

I CAN'T BELIEVE IT... I THOUGHT SHE WAS A LOVELY KITTY CAT.

THERE, THERE, EUGENE. YOU WEREN'T TO KNOW.

OH, COME ON. SHE OOZES EVILNESS.

GLAD TO SEE YOU'RE ALL GETTING ALONG, 'CAUSE YOU'RE GONNA BE IN HERE FOR A REEEEALLY LONG TIME!

EEEEHEHEHEHEE!

SLAM
LOCK
CLICK
LOCK
CLICK
LOCK

YEP, THAT'S MY COUSIN, ALL RIGHT.

EVIL EMPEROR PENGUIN

LAURA ELLEN ANDERSON

IN: RAINBOWS TO THE RESCUE

PARP

OH, EUGEEEENE!

NOT SORRY...

FOR THE LOVE OF CAT'S CRADLE...

GAG

I CAN'T BREATHE!

ARRRGH!

I CAN'T BELIEVE THAT CUTE LITTLE KITTEN I FOUND TURNED OUT TO BE AN EVIL KITTY.

WHAT'S EVIL MASTER GOING TO DO WHEN HE FINDS OUT SHE STOLE ALL HIS SPAGHETTI HOOPS?!

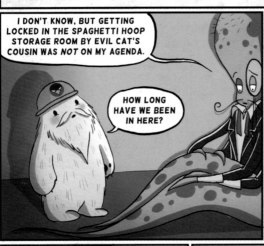

I DON'T KNOW, BUT GETTING LOCKED IN THE SPAGHETTI HOOP STORAGE ROOM BY EVIL CAT'S COUSIN WAS *NOT* ON MY AGENDA.

HOW LONG HAVE WE BEEN IN HERE?

LONG ENOUGH TO BE HAVING SOME FACIAL HAIR ISSUES.

I STILL CAN'T BELIEVE EVILYN OUTWITTED ME!

JUST WAIT 'TIL I GET MY PAWS ON THAT STUPID LITTLE COUSIN OF MINE!

THERE'S NO POINT IN WASTING YOUR ENERGY GETTING ANGRY WITH EVILYN RIGHT NOW.

ERGH, FINE.

I HATE IT WHEN AN OCTOPUS IS RIGHT.

IT DOESN'T SIT WELL WITH ME.

EVIL EMPEROR PENGUIN

Laura Ellen Anderson

IN: I WILL CRECHE YOU - PART 1

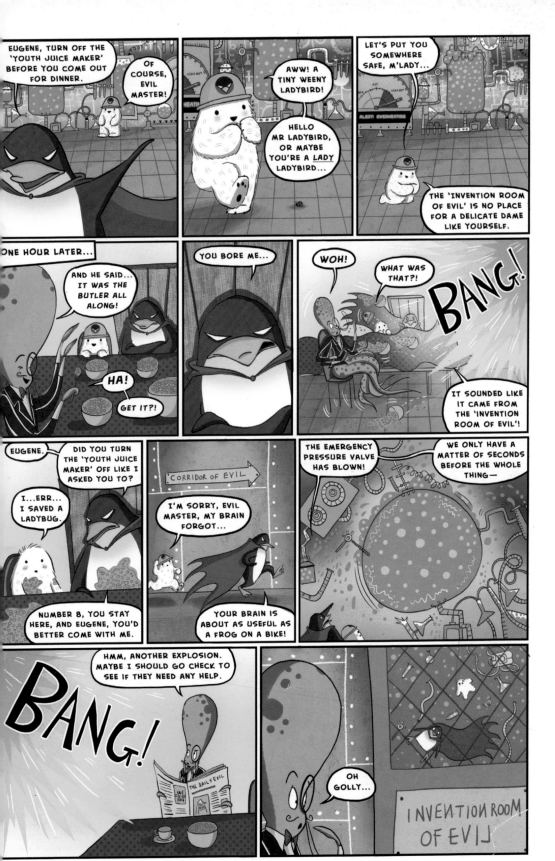

TIME TO USE YOUR TENTACLE TALENTS, NUMBER 8...

DETENTION ROOM OF EVIL

SPLOSH!

WHAT ON EARTH HAPPENED HERE?!

YOU'VE BEEN COMPLETELY SUBMERGED IN 'YOUTH JUICE'!

AT LEAST THE 'DE-AGEFIER' POWER PACK IS STILL INTACT. NOW WHAT ARE WE GOING TO DO WITH YOU TWO?!

BIG PURPLE BLOB!!!

TEE HEE!

OI! HEY, WHAT'RE YOU DOING?!

TAG!

YOU'RE 'IT'!

HEE HEE, YOU CAN'T CATCH ME!!!

NO! WAIT! GET BACK HERE!

WAIT UP!

THE BIG PURPLE BLOB WILL NEFFA CATCH US, EUBEEN!

NEFFA, EFFA, NOT EFFA! TEE HEE HEE!

BOMP!

WELL, WELL, WELL.

HELLO, KIDS...

EVIL EMPEROR PENGUIN

LAURA ELLEN ANDERSON

IN: I WILL CRECHE YOU - PART 2

PREVIOUSLY ON EEP...

THESE GUYS...

GOT TURNED INTO BABIES...

THEN THIS GUY TURNED UP... (OF COURSE)

LOOKS LIKE WE HAD A LITTLE INVENTION MISHAP, EH?!

TAG!

YOU'VE GOT THE LURGIES!

DON'T TOUCH ME.

LAST ONE TO FINISH THE RACE IS A ROTTEN EGG!

A REALLY SMELLY ONE!

HEY! I DO NOT HAVE THE LURGIES AND I AM CERTAINLY **NOT** A ROTTEN EGG!

YOU CAN'T OUTRUN EVIL CAT!

GET BACK HERE!

AAAARGH... WHERE DID THEY GO?!

BOSH!

FOUND YOU!

WAIT...

YOU?!

AREN'T YOU PLEASED TO SEE ME, EIGHT?

NO! OF COURSE NOT!

AND THAT'S NUMBER 8 TO YOU!

HOW DID YOU GET IN HERE?

THROUGH THE FRONT DOOR... DUUUH!

EUGENE, GIVE BACK THE MONOCLE. IT MAKES ME LOOK IMPORTANT.

MONOCLE!

EUGENE! YOU'RE A GENIUS!

I CAN SLIDE THE LOCK OPEN WITH IT!

YES! IT'S WORKING!

LET'S GET OUR EVIL MASTER BACK!

I'M WEEING!

SO, *THIS* WAS YOUR LATEST PLAN THEN, EH?!

THIS INFORMS ME THAT THE LONGER I BLAST SOMEONE WITH THIS THING, THE YOUNGER THEY GET.

SO SURELY, IF I BLAST YOU... YOU'LL NO LONGER EXIST!

I'M SURE THERE'S JUST ENOUGH JUICE IN HERE TO FINISH YOU OFF...

NOW, HOW DOES THIS THING WORK...?

I KNOW *EXACTLY* WHERE THAT RAT OF A CAT WILL BE!

CAT!

SAY GOODBYE TO YOUR EXISTENCE, TINY BIRD!

CLICK

NOOOOOOO!

SPLAT!

MEW.

WELL, WHADDAYA KNOW! THE DE-AGEIFIER DIDN'T WORK PROPERLY ANYWAY.

WHO'D HAVE THOUGHT, SIR, THAT YOUR FAILED ATTEMPT AT WORLD DOMINATION WOULD SAVE YOUR LIFE!

NOW I JUST NEED TO FIGURE OUT A PLAN TO CHANGE YOU BACK...

I WANNA PULL THE KITTY'S WHISKERS OFF!

THIS WAS EASIER SAID THAN DONE...

I WANNA HUG HIM FOREVER!

EVIL EMPEROR PENGUIN

LAURA ELLEN ANDERSON

IN: EUGENE'S DAY OFF

COCKADOODLE DOOOOOOO!!!

WHAT A GLORIOUS MORNING!

YAAAWN

OH MY! IT'S MY DAY OFF TODAY!

I HAVE SO MANY LOVELY THINGS TO DO!

I HOPE EVIL MASTER WILL BE OKAY WITHOUT ME...

I COULD MAYBE HELP A BIT...

HMMM, BUT IT'S THE ONLY DAY OFF I'LL HAVE FOR THE NEXT FIFTEEN YEARS...

ERGH. WHAT A HORRIBLE MORNING.

HMMM, WHAT'S ON TODAY'S AGENDA...

WAIT A MINUTE...

DIARY OF EVIL DATES

KEEP OUT!

EEP

IT'S EUGENE'S DAY OFF!

OKAY, LET'S DO THIS!

TODAY ALREADY SUCKS.

OOO, DAY OFF MEANS PANCAKES FOR BREAKFAST!

PANCAKES INITIATED

EVIL PRINTER PANCAKES ARE THE BEST.

NEILL!

WHERE'S MY BREAKFAST?!

EUGENE REQUESTED YOU AS HIS MINION REPLACEMENT FOR THE DAY... PROVE YOUR WORTH!

HERE WE GO, EVIL MASTER!

I'M SO HONOURED TO BE TOP MINION FOR THE DAY!

BANG!

I THINK THE HASH BROWNS ARE READY...

THIS IS THE PERFECT TIME TO GIVE MY HAT A NICE BIG POLISH TO MAKE IT EXTRA SHINY!

POLISH OF EVIL

HMMM, IT'S 'CAPE OF EVIL WASHING DAY' TODAY... I WONDER IF EVIL MASTER WILL NEED SOME HELP?

OH, SILLY ME! OF COURSE NOT!

DING!

KAA-CHING!

NEILL, WE'RE BEHIND ON TODAY'S 'TO DO' LIST.

HAVE YOU FINISHED WASHING MY CAPES OF EVIL YET?!

ALMOST DONE, EVIL MASTER!

THE'RE JUST DRYING...

IS THAT A MINION IN THE DRYER OF EVIL?

MAYBE...

TEN MINUTES LATER...

WHY ARE ALL MY CAPES TINY!

I'M GOING TO DRAW A PICTURE OF MY MOST FAVOURITE THINGS!

EUGENE COLOUR

AAH, JUST PERFECT!

I THINK EVIL MASTER WILL LOVE IT!

I BET NEILL IS HAVING A WONDERFUL TIME HELPING EVIL MASTER.

I CAN'T WAIT TO START HELPING HIM AGAIN TOMORROW!

NEILL! YOU BIG TOE!

WHERE ARE ALL MY SPAGHETTI HOOPS?

THEY'RE NOT IN THE 'SPAGHETTI HOOP STORAGE ROOM'...

I HAVE YOUR BEST INTERESTS AT HEART, EVIL MASTER.

SO I'VE PUT THEM SOMEWHERE *EXTRA* SAFE, SO THAT NOBODY CAN EVER STEAL THEM EVER AGAIN!

AND *WHERE* EXACTLY WOULD THAT BE?

SPACE!

WHAT?!

SEE! BEST INTERESTS AT...

HEART!

THIS WAS *NOT* ON TODAY'S AGENDA!!!

EUGENE WOULD HAVE HAD THEM STACKED IN ROWS OF THREE 'N' EVERYTHING... THEY WOULDN'T BE IN SPACE!

NEILL, YOU DID PUT EXTRA FUEL IN THE *FLYING POD OF EVIL*, RIGHT?

CHUG CHUG CHUG

WAS I MEANT TO DO THAT *BEFORE* WE LEFT?

GAAAAAAAAH!

HMMM, WHAT LOVELY THING SHALL I DO NEXT?

SMASH

NOW, THAT'S A PRETTY RAINBOW...

OOO, RAINBOW!

I KNOW *JUST* WHAT TO DO NEXT!

94

THIS IS THE PERFECT SPOT FOR A PICNIC, THANKS, KEITH!

ANY TIME, MATEY!

WOULD YOU LIKE TO JOIN MY PICNIC, KEITH?

I HAVE RAINBOW COOKIES!

WELL, I CAN'T SAY NO TO A RAINBOW COOKIE!

I WONDER HOW EVIL MASTER IS DOING...

NO, NEILL, I DO NOT NEED MY OWN THEME TUNE...

I WAS THINKING SOMETHING IN C MINOR... TO MAKE YOU SOUND OMINOUS.

EVIL EMPEROOOOR PENGUIIIIN IS EVIIIIIL! HIS CAPE IS RED, THAT'S WHAT I SAID, OH YEEEEH!

NEVER DO THAT AGAIN.

NOW, FOCUS!

THIS INVENTION IS *HIGHLY* EXPLOSIVE, SO WE HAVE TO BE EXTRA CAREFUL UNTIL IT HAS BEEN PLANTED DEEP UNDER THE ATLANTIC OCEAN...

SO *DO NOT*, UNDER ANY CIRCUMSTANCES, PULL THE RED WIRE.

OH... YOU MEAN, THIS ONE?

I'M SURE HE'S DOING FINE WITHOUT ME.

BOOM!

GEOFFREY CERTAINLY DIDN'T SEE THAT ONE COMING!

GET READY TO HOLD YOUR SIDES!

Squid Bits!

Squidgy!

Squid Bits!

They're tentacool!

by Jess Bradley

Poot!

Hello!

Cluck.

Clock.

CLUNK.

MonsterFashion! Looking good to scare good!

The Sassy Gill-Man

Water-related colour scheme a must

Keep those gills perky

Under-arm webbing is all the rage in France

Take care of those scales

Swimming trunks add a sporty look

Another great accessory: A few strands of kelp can add that touch of yuck!

This place is starting to feel a bit fishy!

The Department of Awesome Vehicles

The Fish Scooter.

Create Some Doodle Doods!

Whoop!

I want that cake...

've got the est view rom here!

very long

Morceaux de Calmer

Squid Bits!

They're tentacool!

by Jess Bradley

1 Squid Bits SQUISHY MONEY 1 Squid Bits

✂ Cut out and Spend—
Squid Bits Currency! *

Woo! Shooting Star! Make a Wish!

Eat more Vitamin R

Yummy! I ♥ radishes!

* Not Worth anything—not real money

Totally Real Nature Guide

Giant Oboe Crab

These huge crabs inhabit most Shorelines angrily waving about their oboes which, due to their Over-sized claws, they Cannot play.

Squid Bits!

I say!

Everyone knows that Squid Bits was established in 1862 - Let's travel back and see how one of the earlier strips looked!

The Steam-Driven Guinea Pig

An Operator's Guide

≥ Centennial Edition! ≤

Professor Possum's Honest-to-Goodness Squid Tonic!

Maker of the Medicine Hammer

Cures Most Ailments!*

- Gurgles from the bottom
- Crazy Foot
- Vampirism (mild to full)
- Itching caused by ghosts
- Sloth Fever
- Mirror Madness
- Velocipede Rash

*May cause more ailments

Ornamental Animals!

Perfect for your domicile

The Table-Side Pig

A lovely decoration for the parlour or day room.

The Fireside Lap Dolphin.

What could make your evening more relaxing than your very own Lap Dolphin! New and elegant.

The Curiosity Cabinet

Behold! The Dog-Faced Dog!

Does anyone fancy a using game of Pac-man?

Sounds delightful but video games haven't been invented yet!

Red Panda's Insult Guide ☆

Has someone called you a cad or a bounder? Try some of these Spiffing responses!

- You, sir, reek of flatulence.
- Verily, you are rather awful.
- I suggest you go sweep a chimney.
- I find the arrangement of your face baffling.

I do profess that I like very little, including you, the reader.

 I say, do you like my new hat?

 It's fine, but I prefer mine!

 Say, what do you make of all this w-fangled electrical nonsense?

I couldn't possibly comment.

 Then I will ask this fine gentleman of upstanding intelligence. What do you think, good sir?

 Banana.

Gasp!

By Jove, he's right!

 Clap! clap! Clap!

Good Show!

What wit!

Genius!

Brilliant!

Squid Bits!

They're tentacool!

by Jess Bradley

Offended Animals ☆

No, I'm not good at D.I.Y.!

Hee hee!

Octopus Crossing

Squid Bits balloons! Only £1 each!

Squid Bits Cut'n'keep Characters!
Fill in the Speech bubbles!

A Day in the life of a Cow

o's gone and cked all of mud in?!

Join me in a bowl of Tom Yum Soup!

7:00 am Munch munch!

12:00pm Munch munch!

16:00pm Munch munch!

19:00pm Munch munch!

22:30pm Why did I leave it so late to start this essay?!

It's due tomorrow!

How is business?

Under Control!

Business is good, Sir!

No probs!

Hmm, good. keep it up.

THIS IS BUSINESS!

107

Squid Bits!

kiwi wee wee!

They're tentacool!

by Jess Bradley

Totally Real Nature Guide.

Stinky_kelp_Gull

The Stinky kelp Gull grows a crest and tail of kelp and constantly smells like low tide. Watch out for their bright green poo that reeks of fish.

I'm a Computer! I know everything!

Do you know what love is?

...no.

Squid Bits: Poetry Slam!

My kiwi

has done a wee wee.

My computer says hi to me when I log on!

You broke it, you bought it!

I can smell that gull from here!

The Red Panda: nature's JERK

Pottery Shop.

This looks rubbish!

Poke!

CRASH! SMASH!

Tinkle

Whoops.

My Pottery!!

Ah, it's finally spring! How wonderful!

I feel alive! What a lovely spring breeze!

What...? No! MY FACE!!

wind!

ROBERT!!

Squid Bits!

Bleebledegrunt!

They're tentacool!

by Jess Bradley

Birds with Swords!

- Have at thee!

I'm quite skilled with the épée!

My sound effect is Wuuurbett!

I f-eel great!

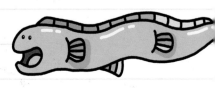

Official Words for Everyday Sounds!

Gweent. — Hee! gweent! The sound of a sea cucumber guffing.

Blarmpf. Blarmpf! The sound of a bear accidentally swallowing his chewing gum.

Zurnglebump. Help!! Zurnglebump! The sound of a crab in a box falling down the stairs.

Make up your own sound effect!

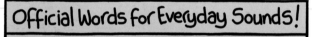

111

FOR A VERY BIG LAUGH!

FOR YOUR OWN CRITTER TITTER, SIMPLY READ...

Gary's Garden

I'm going in after him!

No, Harriet. Don't be stupid.

Oh, what is he doing? I can't bear it!

He's been gone so long!

Wait! There he is! There he is!

What's he got in his beak?

Fly, Clarence, FLY!

CREAK!

Flap Flap Flap

Someone's coming!

What did you get?

What is it?

Who knows? They're sure sweet and sticky, though.

Let me try one!

Me too!

Wassisface has finally gotten round to putting the crusts out.

Let him. I'm eating these now.

Chomp!

Old Podgy the pigeon can fill his boots!

You know what? That place was FULL of CRAZY stuff!

Chew!

Slurp!

Never have I laid my eyes on such wonders before...

Packets of golden worms, jars of squidgy fruit...

Wow! Golden Worms!

I want me some of them!

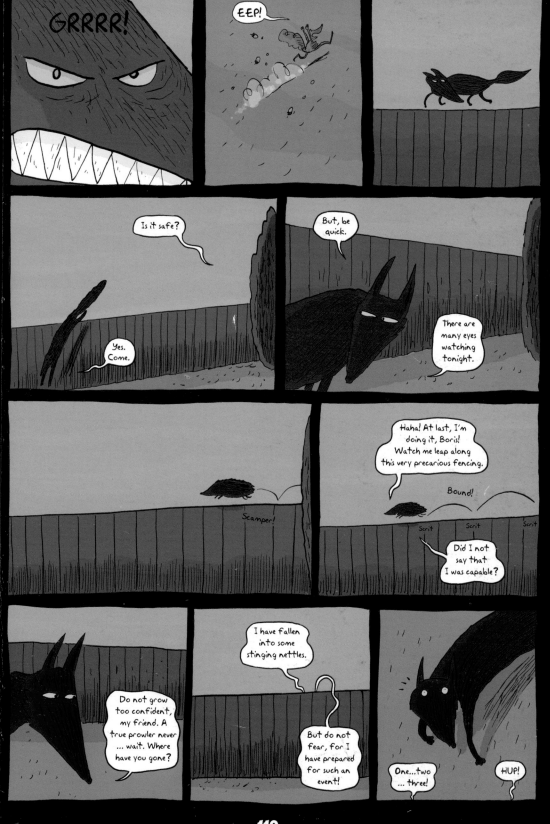

Gary's Garden

By Gary Northfield

Yawn!

Good morning, world!

Oh, wow! It's the anniversary of the day I found my very first acorn!

I painted it gold and everything!

I still treasure it till this very day.

SCREAM!! It's gone!

Who would do such a thing?!

I remember the day I found my acorn so clearly.

Mama! I gots one! I gots one!

I gots an acorn!

My Mama was so pleased.

Look Mama!

Oh Rupert, it's wonderful!

Your Papa would've been so proud.

Now we need to paint it gold and treasure it to remind you of today!

...Papa...

Garden creatures! Heed my words!

Your days of freedom are numbered. Soon my Evil Empire shall reign supreme and all will bow before me!

So sayeth DARTH LADYBIRD!

Ooh! Is there going to be an Evil Empire?

Will we get ray guns?

How exciting!

Why is he wearing a stupid acorn on his head?

He looks like an idiot!

Imbecile!

I find your lack of faith disturbing!

But, what's this...?

I sense something... The Force is strong in this one...

Who me?

How marvellous!

Oi!

Is that my Golden Acorn on your head?

Give it back you weirdo!

?

This is not the acorn that you're looking for...

What?! Yes it is!

Hey! have you cut eye holes in it?

Foul creature!

Prepare to meet your doom!

Twist!

VWOOM!

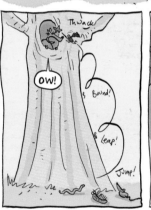

Thwack!

OW!

Bound!

Leap!

Jump!

Ow!

Ow!

Ow!

Ow!

Get off!

Noooo!

Thwack!

Rupert...

We could've ruled the Galaxy together...

Are you all right?

Yes... I have fallen on a worm...

Can I have my acorn back now?

Noooo! None must gaze at my hideous face!

What about MY face? You're sitting on it!

Your face does not concern me worm, for I am DARTH LADYBIRD!

Sigh...

Gary's Garden

By Gary Northfield

Previously in Gary's Garden...

Larry Ladybird's girlfriend is missing...

She is to marry Dracula?!

NOOOOO!

Larry and Chompy battle strange creatures in a strange land...

AAAIIEE!!

Chomp!

They meet a ladybird who calls himself, Colin The Barbarian...

Ooh, doesn't he have lovely hair?

Gasp!

Explain yourselves strangers, you are not welcome in these lands!

Wait! We come in peace! We seek the lair of Dracula, servant of Evil!

So exciting! A real barbarian!

I've always dreamed of being a barbarian!

The fiend has stolen the girl I love...

...Love ... yes ... I have heard of this word..

Ooh. He's gone into a trance. Are you all right there, Colin?

This way!

Cor! Off he goes! What a hero!

Wait!

Come on, Chompy! We have to go!

All right, all right. Wait up!

And so!

There, the tree stump yonder. Here you will find your foe.

Phew! Is it far? I'm a bit tired!

Tired?! How can you be tired??

Gulp!

When you have battled the Red Horde of the Damned while carrying four of your injured brethren across perilous fields for three days, THEN and only then come to me with your tales of tiredness!

Groan!

Gah!

124

Cor, how rude! Who rattled his cage?

Quiet, weakling! We must make haste!

Leap!

Chompy?! Why do you speak to me in such tones? Why are you wearing moss on your head?

I've decided to become a barbarian like Colin. Do you like my new hair?

It looks like a bird has pooed on your head.

Come, my friend.

Soon

We must tread cautiously - many dark and terrible creatures hide near the Stump of Dracula.

YOU can be cautious, but Golden Hair is in that black tower and I can't wait any longer.

Wait, reckless one!

Bah, your friend runs with his heart and not his head. His foolishness will be his undoing.

Yes, many times I have asked him to look deep into his soul and search for the true answers. But perhaps only true barbarians are capable of such insight.

You are an odd fellow.

t Dracula's Stump!

ARGH!

Put me down!

There is a mad man at our door!

Where is Golden Hair, villains?

Get the boss, quick!

Larry? Is that you?

Golden Hair?!

AAAIEE!

I have found you!

Quick, we must flee!

I'm not fleeing! Why are you here? Did you not find my letter?

Yes! But I assumed it to be false, written by the hand of Dracula, servant of Evil. I am here to rescue you!

Is there a problem, Elaine darling?

See, Larry? He calls me Elaine!

Oh! Is this the fellow you mentioned before? Lovely to meet you, old boy. I've heard all about you.

Oh.

He may be a Servant of Evil, Larry, but Dracula treats me with respect and dignity.

Yeah, but can he imitate the call of an ELEPHANT?! AAROOGA! No, I thought not!

Larry, Please...

Who will save you from rampaging crocodiles? Not this villainous fool.

Who is great at opening jars of pickles? This weakling? Thought not.

Stop it.

And so

I'm sorry my friend, you have a noble heart, she just cannot see it.

Better to have loved and lost, than never loved at all. That is the barbarian's way...

Sigh.

Are all caterpillars this strange in your land?

No... just this one...

Oi! I am here you know!

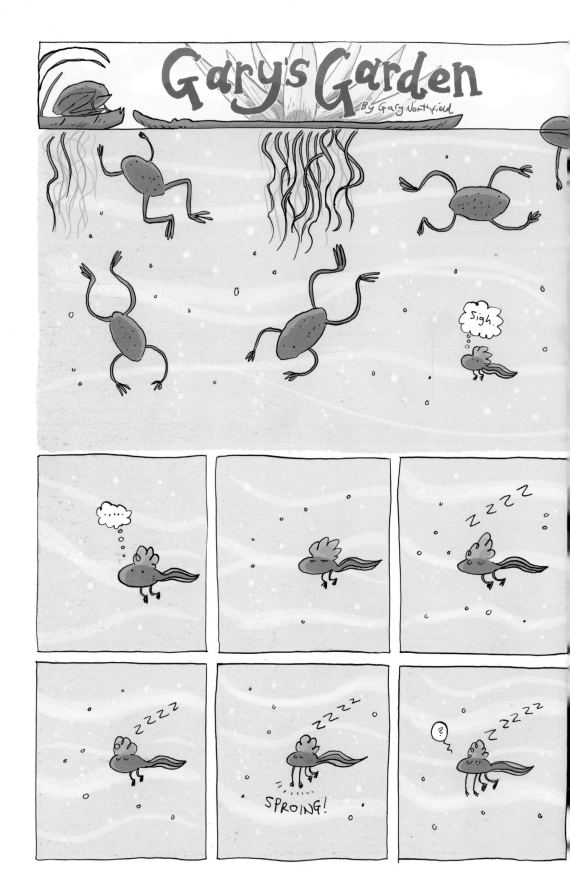

Gary's Garden

By Gary Northfield

Hello and welcome, one and all...

To this month's ART CLASS!

Here, I hope you will learn the incredible skills that will take you on a path of personal expression and internal discovery.

'Scuse me! 'Scuse me!

Yes, yes. What is it?

Will we be learning how to do shading? I'm rubbish at shading.

Yeah, and cars. I can't draw cars!

No! There will be no shading, no drawing of cars!

Art is about seeing the unseeable.

?

We will be drawing the landscapes of your mind!

For our first exercise, you will be drawing our model, Marcel, with your eyes closed!

What?!

That's ridiculous!

Excuse me, but how are we meant to see what we're drawing if we have our eyes closed?

I don't get it.

I want you to throw off your mental shackles, Mr Slug. Forget everything you know.

We are expanding your realms. Redefining your creativity.

You mustn't rely on simple eyesight alone for art.

Sob! I just want to paint pretty watercolours!

Get drawing, everyone. Come, come!

Boohoo-hoo!

See the shapes in your mind's eye...

Imagine the contours forming in the air.

Who is Marcel? What is his purpose?

Draw that purpose!

Magnificent, Mr Slug. Magnificent!

Remarkable, in fact.

Really? Uf! Can I see?

Yes, do! Everyone open your eyes!

Oh.

Er...

And that's 'good', is it?

Ha ha! Let's see yours! Mine's a right mess!

I'm not sure what's going on any more.

I want to go home...

Mr Wasp, I couldn't help notice that you had your eyes open.

Grr.

No, no! That's good! Carry on!

Bravo, one and all! For our next exercise I want you to draw Marcel with your eyes open....

And with Marcel moving every ten seconds.

Eh?

This is stupid.

When are we going to start drawing properly? I paid a lot of money for this class!

Mr Slug!

Release yourself from your box! Discard your blinkers! Open your sluggy mind!

THE END!

Gary's Garden

By Gary Northfield

Colouring by Lisa Murphy!

Laydeez and Gentleslugs... Introducing...

STUNT SLUG!

Yay!

Whoop!

Woo!

Stunt Slug!!
Stunt Slug!!
Stunt Slug!!

Drumroll!!

Ooh! Exciting!

Drumroll!

Where is he?

This is rubbish.

Drumroll!

Boo!

Boo!

We want Stunt Slug!

Cymbol clash!

plop!

There he is!

That was quite the entrance.

Well, he is a Stunt Slug.

Thank you! Thank you!

And may I present to you...

my lovely assistant ...

Geraldine!

Woo!

Yeah!

Sparkly!

Gary's Garden

By Gary Northfield

Welcome, contestants, to this year's **GREAT GARDEN BAKE OFF!**

In front of you, you will find all the ingredients you will need for a classic leaf pie!

You have half an hour in which to bake a beautiful pie with which to wow us judges.

cough

Does anyone have any questions?

Yes, I do.

I seem to have been stuck next to a disgusting stinky fly. I'd like to move, please.

?

Well, how rude.

I'll have you know I'm a chef of great renown!

What of? Poo pies?

Hmph.

Um... Jake, do you mind swapping with Rowena?

Eh?

Why have I got to move? I don't wanna be next to a smelly fly neither!

I'm sorry Rowena. I'm afraid you're just going to have to stay put for now.

Hph.

Ridiculous.

OK! If we're all ready?

Let's get BAKING!

Stir! Stir!

Sweat! Sweat!

Plop!

Slop!

Hello Jake! Would you like to talk us through your pie?

?

Sprinkle

Well I've pureed the twigs into a nice paste.

Then I've stirred in crumbly dry leaves to create a gratin crust.

Yum.

Lovely.

And will you be topping it off with a garnish of weeds plucked from the garden?

Yes. Yes I will.

Your wig looks like a garnish of weeds picked from the garden...

Yeah, well, your face resembles a gratin crust from where I'm sitting...

And Rowena, what's your approach to this classic bake?

Oh... erm... hahaha

Er... I've put in some leaves and er twigs...

Scribble Scribble

And I'll be er... enveloping it in a.... um.... futon... of bark...

Wait, isn't a futon a sort of sofa bed?

It is?

Wonderful! I love the humour in this piece! Let's hope this 'futon' doesn't cushion the blow of the flavours.

Rasp

Ha Ha HA!

Bah!

And Vanessa, would you care to describe your pie?

Um... right. I've er... taken a deck chair of er... leaves and um...

A deck chair?!

Oh yeah, sorry, I mean a pouf cushion of leaves, and posted it in an envelope of mud.

Right.

That just sounds stupid.

Ha ha! 'Deckchair'! I think we know who's going to be winning this Bake Off!

Hmph.

Psst! Mum! Hey Mum!

?

What are you making?

Are you winning?

Shoo! Go away! No kids allowed!

Where's your brother, Robbie? I told you all to stick together.

We lost him.

We thought he was with you.

No, he's not with me!

Now, go and find him, or there'll be no dinner tonight.

OK, everyone – put down your spoons!

Mm... This pie is delicious, Jake.

The crumbly leaves are the winner here.

Slurp!

And Vanessa, your... um Deckchair and envelope ensemble...

I don't think the consistency is there. Do you?

Er... 'Spose not.

Sniff Sniff

Yuk.

And finally, Rowena. I LOVE, LOVE your humour!

Pop!

So tasty!

?

BOO!

Arr!! A maggot!!

That is so disgusting! EVERYONE'S DISQUALIFIED! This kitchen is shut down!

Robbie?

Bleugh! I ate some of that!

Glub! I need a raspberry compote to hide the taste!

I'm sorry, Mum... Did I do wrong?

Nah, you did good, son. Fancy an envelope of mud?

A what?

The end!

Gary's Garden

By Gary Northfield

Welcome one and all to this month's Rock Club.

I see we have quite the selection to discuss.

Who would like to begin?

Well, I'd like to talk to you all about my calcium sulphate dihydrate.

A prized rock, given to me by my dear papa.

UNTRUTH! It was I, not your father, who lent you that rock many moons ago. In fact, I thought it lost.

I shall require that you return it to me FORTHWITH!

Unhand my ore! It's mine and mine alone!

I'm afraid you are incorrect in your declaration!

Sirs! Let me resolve this trifle!

Gasp!

Who??

PLOP

I think you'll find your sparkling gem is now MY property!

Who dares?

Farewell, chums!

Don't be sad!

Your trinkets will make some paupers glad!

'Trinkets'? My calcium sulfate dihydrate is no mere 'trinket'!

So ... erm ... ahem. It appears that today's meeting is at an end.

Shall we meet again next week?

Minus the frivolities, one hopes.

Bah!

I'm joining Twig Club...

Leap!

Meanwhile.

♪

You, green worm!

Do you prosper?

Eh?

?

Are you well-heeled? Flush? Loaded? Well-to-do?

What say you?

What are you on about?

ARE YOU RICH?

Er ... no. Not really.

Then you shall wear this beautiful stone on your head.

Plonk!

?

I think I like it!

FEEL THE POWER OF FOOD INSPIRED LAUGHTER! NOM NOM - HE HE!

BOOKS ARE NOT GOOD SOURCES OF VITAMINS AND MINERALS, THEY ARE, HOWEVER, EXCELLENT SOURCES OF **LAUGHTER**...

GOREBRAH!

Puff! Pant!

THE LAST BISCUIT IS MINE!!

YOU ARE INCORRECT ABOUT BISCUITS!!

MEGA-INHALATION!

AWESOME Biiiiscuitsss!!!

HYPER BELCH!

CRUMPLE!

Urg, my head! Where was I?

Well, there you have it, folks, only the mightiest warriors snack on Awesome Biscuits!

Pffft! You're using a tree for a microphone!

This is Gorebrah, reporting from the pile of slushy ice that used to be a glacier full of legendary ancient biscuits. Back to you in the studio! BARBARIAN APPÉTIT!

GOREBRAH!

MAKING CAKES WITH THE STRENGTH OF A HUNDRED BAKERS!

Salutations, Readers! You might be wondering what I'm doing. Well...

We're climbing a beanstalk!

But... why, Gorebrah?

Ahhh... that's easy, little Sam...

...to reach this giant castle! So, today's recipe has an interesting twist, because instead of...

Gorebrah, could you explain everything after we reach the top?

Oh, because of your tiny, tired arms, of course!

One strenuous climb later...

Here we are! Now, for today's recipe. I'll be using a different set of muscles than usual...

This one...

And this one! For we will be making...

148

A MILKSHAKE INFUSED WITH THE LAUGHTER OF A PRINCESS!!

Parp Par Par Paaaarp!!

Parp Par Par Paaaarp!!

Every year, the princess invites comedians from all over the kingdom to make her laugh with jokes and goofs.

Whoever elicits the most chuckles is rewarded with a delicious ice-cream treat, sweetened by the SWEETEST laughter in the land!

And... you're going to be telling jokes?

Yup. I'm going to be slaying them with my zingers and also some tomfoolery.

This will be very easy. Probably my most effortless recipe yet...

PARP!

I'm sorry, Gorebrah. I just don't see you as the comedy type...

Nonsense! I know jokes, I have the best jokes!

Did you hear the one about the poultry, and its decision-making in regards to road safety?

Yeah...that's a good one...

In the Princess's throne room...

Send in the next contender!

Don't you even have any notes?

Nope. I like to wing it. I was born funny. AND muscular!

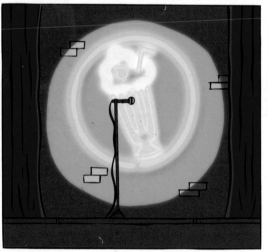

Greetings! How doth everyone feel this eve?

Um...hello my...lady... f...fair....lady...

150

So....what is the deal with... with... furry pants? Right?

Sure, they keep you warm... but why so itchy?

Huh? Am I right?

Right?

Oh no.

BOO!

SPLUP!

BOOO!!

This was a silly idea. let's go home...

I thought we were going to make a milkshake. What's this?

BOO!!

Change of plan. I made you tomato juice... just drink it.

...snigger!

HAHAHA! HAHAHA HAAHAA!!

Gorebrah... You've still got it!

GOREBRAH!

Discovering the strangest dishes in the Universe, every week!

OK, everyone, the burgers will be ready soon!

Oh no. Is that thunder?

Hmm...no. It sounds more like...horses pulling a chariot?

CLOSE! IT WAS A GIANT HIPPO!

SMASH!

GRUH!

My goodness, that's one brawny barbarian!

It's Gorebrah, the chef that fed a thousand universes!

Yes, that is a big thing that I did!

So...you smashed down my garden fence because...??

I was taking my hippo for a gallop and noticed you were having a barbecue... Are these burgers? Very nice... but what if, instead, we cooked...

THINGS WE FORAGE FROM THIS MYSTERIOUS DUNGEON??

YES!

What?

Grab your foraging basket and come with me, little Callie! Who knows what we will find down there?

Or what it'll taste like!

HEY!!

Slurp!

Gorebrah. I can't see a thing!

Hmmm... I have an idea!

I brought my glow-in-the-dark crown! Limited Edition!

Neat!

Squeak!

Squeak!

Squeak!

LOOK, CALLIE! SUCCULENT SMOKY SAUSAGE BATS! GRAB THEM!

SAUSAGE BATS??

And look! They've uncovered a bounty of Chilli-con-crystals!

Squeak!

So shiny! AND spicy!

I am a troll! Foll-de-roll!

Greetings, troll, foll-de-roll. We come from the surface world in search of edible treasures.

What price do you ask for a basket full of your precious Chilli-con-crystals?

If my crystals it is ye seek, then challenge me, but be not weak! My weapon of choice may make you bristle...

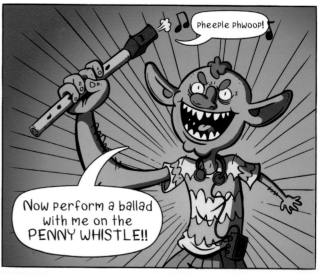

Pheeple phwoop!

Now perform a ballad with me on the PENNY WHISTLE!!

I'm sorry, Mr Troll, but I don't think either of us know how to play the penny whistle...

Oh...well... that's ok... perhaps I could teach you?

OK!!

Any sign of them?

No... but I hear a terrible whistling sound. I assume that's them...

Terrible sound...

One intensive wind instrument lesson later...

...and a troll's waistcoat must always be... ironed!!

PWEEEP!!

154

Yeah, let's do another one! Let's do something that really cooks!

That sounds fun, whistle-troll. But we've got to get back home. We're having a barbecue!

Oh well, if you ever want to jam again, you know where I am... in this stinking dungeon!

Ok, bye!

Oh, wait. I almost forgot about our final ingredient...

Do we have to cross an invisible bridge in order to gain a delicious bread that gives us x-ray vision??

No. It's just this slime. You can eat it. It tastes ok.

Oh.

GREETINGS, FAMILY! WE HAVE TRIUMPHED OVER THE MYSTERIOUS BARBECUE DUNGEON AND RETURN WITH THE +5 CHILLI-DOG OF DIVINE NOURISHMENT!!

Oh, that's good timing!

What do you... OH NO!!!

We've just ran out of potato salad and your hippo did NOT take it well...

NO! CHAMBOURCY! BAD HIPPO!!

BARBARIAN APPÉTIT!

Gorebrah bumps into an old rival, but can they work together long enough to make a healthy meal for the kids?

Cooking you the WEIRDEST dishes in the world. every week!

One day, in Polly and Michael's kitchen...

Oh no, the cakes are ruined!!

Now what are we going to do?

NEVER FEAR! GOREBRAH IS HERE TO CHASE AWAY YOUR BAKING NIGHTMARES! BEGONE TASTY PHANTASMS!!

CRASH

My commiserations, Polly and Michael. Baking is not easy. It took me years and many muscles to perfect my cake skills.

But what if you helped me to create the sweetest, stickiest, chocolatiest cake that has ever been created?

YEAH!

SPECTACULAR! The first step is to put on these hats!

CAKEWARD HO!

SMASH!

Keep the noise down in there, you two!

Quite soon, deep in the jungle...

So, it is here, in the deepest, sugariest part of the jungle where we hunt for the Cocoa Caribe!

Or, as some call it, the Chocolate Piranha!

Be careful. Its teeth are delicious, but they are also very sharp!

Be careful. It may look delicious, but it will rot your teeth in seconds!

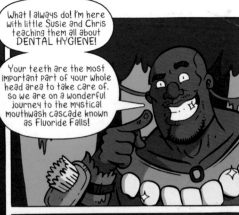

What I always do! I'm here with little Susie and Chris teaching them all about DENTAL HYGIENE!

Your teeth are the most important part of your whole head area to take care of, so we are on a wonderful journey to the mystical mouthwash cascade known as Fluoride Falls!

Brusheryn the Gleaming?

Gorebrah the... Gorebrah?

BUMP!

What are you doing here?

That is the stupidest thing I've ever heard.

Humph! No wonder it's of no interest to YOU, Gorebrah!

What do you mean by that?

Didn't they have braces in your realm? A parrot could fly through the gap in your teeth!

WHISTLE!

Yes, well, you have... the... your... um...

Ha HA!

SLAP!

Ugh! So slimy! And bad for my tooth enamel!

Avast, ye brute!

GRAHH!

TUSSLE!

157

BRUSHA! BRUSHA! BRUSHA!

ARRGHH! MY BURLY GUMS!

Both of you, stop! This is giant barbarian madness!!

Guh?

The children are right, Brusheryn. We are mighty champions, we should not squabble like tiny champions.

True. We are here for a greater purpose: to share our immense wisdom with the children!

Is there not a way for us to combine your mastery of the delicious with my dental wholesomeness?

By the splendour of our rippling biceps, we will find a way, my friend!

YAYYY!! THIS IS GOING TO BE AWESOME!!

Hmmm... I'm not sure...

SIEVE!

Something's not right...

CRACK!

flour

STIR!

...but I can't put my finger on it...

158

OK, there it is.

SQUIRT!

12:00

This was a mistake...

SQUIRRRT!

GOREBRAH AND BRUSHERYN'S Fudgey-Toothpaste-Sundae! With a minty stripe!

I think we probably should have let them carry on fighting...

Who wants the first piece?

Maybe YOU should try a slice, Gorebrah?

Huh?

You know, because of your breath...

It smells like gravy and beef!

THEY ARE THE TWO BEST SMELLS!

SMASH!

See? What did I tell you? Problem solved!

Brush your teeth! BRUSH THEM!!

SUGAR RULES!!

GOREBRAH!

OK, we've got pasta, tomatoes, cucumber, onion. What's next?

PASTA

CRASH!

Need a hand making pasta salad? I'm the Master of Pasta!

GOREBRAH!

We're trying to make this, Gorebrah, can you help?

Of course. Let's just see what...

Oh no...

OH NO!

OH GNOME!

RECIPE CORNER!
GNOME PASTA SALAD

FRESH GNOME GOSSIP
HÖRK'S NEW ALBUM! "It's my BEST album yet!"

NART'S NEW HAT! "It's my BEST hat yet!"

The recipe says that the only way to make it properly is to go to the gnome village. Will you take us there to see how it's made, Gorebrah?

Please?

GNOME TALK

Certainly not. Every time I go to the gnome village they always make me do embarrassing things...

...which I secretly enjoy because of my gentle artistic soul...

UUUHHHHHH

PLEEEEASE, GOREBRAH? We love the gnomes, Gorebrah! They're SO cute!

PLEEEASE? We'll be the coolest kids in school, Gorebrah!

Gnomes wear funny hats, Gorebrah!

PLEEEEASE?

Soon, at the gnome village...

GNOMES...

Ooh! Something's happening over there!

Um...hello? Can someone tell us where to find the... Hello??

YOU! Hurry up. You're on stage in five minutes. We need to get you into make-up!

No... you don't understand. We're here to find some...

You're here for the pasta salad.

Yes, but...

Well, we only make it ONE WAY, so we need you in make up NOW!

In the gnome theatre...

So, this is a play all about pasta salad?

Yes! Ye olde gnomes wrote this star-crossed lovers' story to celebrate their most treasured light summer dish!

Ooh, quiet now. It's starting!

Verily, my pasta is dull and without flavour, much like my life!

... Lo... My salad hath many vitamins and minerals...yet none of the carbohydrates that give life its energy!...

Forsooth!

Look, there he is!

Tee hee!

If only, perchance, there were another to share mine excellent recipe with. The recipe of love, and of pasta salad!

clap clap clap clap

Hee hee hee hee!!

clap clap

Thy vegetables are so fresh and green!

The secret is love... and also manure!

Aw. So romantic!

Gasp!

Gasp!

Now. We add this feta cheese. It doth smell strong and quite like feet. but its powerful stench represents my most wondrous love for thee!

Oh. my handsome salad maker. thou art so... Sniff...

Oh yes. that smelleth bad...

Leavest this place. salad maker! My daughter shall not mix with the likes of thee! This is a Pasta Kingdom!

How much longer does this go on for? My tights are itchy!

Forty-five minutes later...

I knew thou woudst return to me. my love. Come. walkest thou through the stinging nettles to my side.

You want me to walk through stinging nettles now??

Nope! This is too silly! I'm not doing it any more!

...but... my love!

What's happening?

I'm not sure. The salad maker must make a great sacrifice. but Gorebrah is going OFF SCRIPT!

But... truly tis selfish to just leave and spoil the work of so many people...

I cannot make others sad just so I feel better... sigh... OK...

I shall walk through the nettles to see thee, my love. I don't care how much those gents will sting mine arms, legs and bum.

Ow! Ouch!

STING STING STING

Mine own darling! We are reunited and our pasta salad wilt ne'er be separated again!

Verily, my legs are all stung up...

Smek!

Pasta salad for all!!

clap clap clap slap

Back home...

So THAT'S how pasta salad was first made! I never knew it would be so romantic!

KYLIE MINGNOME

Mmm! This is delicious! Thank you, Gorebrah. You were brilliant!

Thou art... I mean, you are welcome! I'm just glad this whole thing is over...

However, a few weeks later at the Gnome Awards...

Sob! Gnomes!!

Best actor in a pasta-based performance
GOREBRAH

GOREBRAH!

Cooking you the CREEPIEST dishes in the world, every week!

Somewhere, deep in the Antarctic...

OUTPOST #31 CULINARY SCHOOL

KITCHENS

So, you may be wondering why I've tied you all to your seats...

Yes, that's the main thing that we've all been wondering!

I have reason to believe that one of you is NOT who they seem. That they are in fact A GIANT PRAWN in disguise!

You don't mean...?

YES. One of you is... A SHRIMPOSTER!

Ugh... terrible joke...

A dislike of puns, eh? How very shellfish-like of you!

No...no... it's funny! Hahaha!!! See how I laugh?

Hmm... maybe you should be the first to take my test to find the prawn amongst the men. You're all going to try my seafood bisque!

Oh no, I couldn't possibly.

No, you should, it's quite delicious.

ALSO IT WILL EXPOSE YOU AS THE PRETENDER YOU ARE!

No...please I can't...

SILENCE! SAMPLE MY SOUP!

164

MURHPGH!!

Look! I knew it! He's mutating into his true form!

No, he's actually very allergic to shellfish and he's having a reaction.

UY TURLD YUHW!!!

Ah, well...I'm very sorry about that... But no matter!

Because it means Detective Gorebrah is one step closer to solving the case...

Something's wrong. You're not acting like the Gorebrah we all know and love!

You're crazy! I'm getting out of here!

Running away? Obvious prawn tactics!

TASTE THE SOUP OF TRUTH, MONSTER!!

IT HAS THE FINEST SAFFRON IN IT!!

The few hours I spent imitating you were the happiest and most fulfilling of my life!

LEAP!

Your skill in the kitchen is unmatched and I wanted to know how it felt to bring joy to others through my cooking!

Your seafood bisque smells heavenly! And I respect your desire to grow as both a person and as a chef!

BOUND!

Wait, we're... paying each other compliments instead of battling? Are we... friends?

Yes! POWERFUL friends!

And we must cement this bond with some kind of exquisite, slow-cooked, dish-based meal!

Awww! I thought we were going to watch him fight a monster! Then eat a fancy soup!

Maybe this will be even better?

SPICY ALGAE STEW!

It's the best bacteria-based broth you'll ever taste!

No. This is much worse...

Cooked with friendship! And also algae!

CUN SUMWUN CURL A DOGTURR PLEEEEESH??

PRAWN APPÉTIT!

...This guy!

167

LOOSHKIN

THE CRAZY ADVENTURES OF...

...THE MADDEST CAT IN THE WORLD!

MIAOW!

MIAOW!

HELLOOOOOOO?

HONKK

LOOSHKIN, WHAT ARE YOU DOING? IT'S HALF PAST MIDNIGHT!

I WANT THIS TURTLE TO BE MY FRIEND.

I WILL CALL HIM GARY SQUIRREL!

HUGGGGGGGGGZ

GARY SQUIRREL THE TURTLE.

BUT WE CAN'T HAVE ANY GREAT ADVENTURES IF HE WON'T WAKE UP.

LOOSHKIN, YOU CAN'T FORCE SOMEONE INTO BEING YOUR FRIEND.

FRIENDSHIP COMES FROM HAVING MUTUAL INTERESTS!

YOU'RE RIGHT. I'LL DANCE!!

WHAT, WHEN DID I SAY

LA LA LA

FAH LAH LA LOO LAH LAH

HMM. BETTER JAZZ IT UP A BIT.

STOMPY STOM PLOP PLOP FRRP

STOMPY STOMP

FRRP

SHRIEK!

BOOM! BOOM BOO

WH GO ON?

...LAHHHH!

WHAT ARE YOU DOING HANGING AROUND MY EMPTY SHELL?

GASPP! GARY SQUIRREL.

NO, MY NAME'S...

GARY SQUIRREL!

OH, REALLY? OKAY, COOL.

PLOP!

I JUST NIPPED OUT TO GO TO THE 24-HOUR SUPERMARKET.

BY THE WAY...

WHAT WAS THAT COOL DANCING YOU WERE DOING?

JUST, Y'KNOW. FOUND A CIRCUS.

WELL, IT WAS RAD!

A MUTUAL INTEREST!

NO! NO NO NO!

LOOSHKIN

THE CRAZY ADVENTURES OF...

...THE MADDEST CAT IN THE WORLD!

THIS EPISODE:

THPTHBT THHHH HHHHH HHHHONK!

HOW RUDE.

THPTHBTHHH

HEY, LOOK AT LOOSHKIN! HE'S BEING FUNNY!

THPTHBTHH

WHAT IS IT, BOY? ARE YOU PRETENDING TO RIDE A MOTORBIKE?

HA HA! WHAT A SILLY CAT!

★SLAM!★

HA HA!

THPBTHHHH

WHAT'S WRONG WITH THAT CAT?

LOOSHKIN! MY NEMESIS! WE MEET AGAI... WHERE ARE YOU GOING?

THPTHBTHH

WHAT'S GOING ON? HAVE YOU FINALLY LOST YOUR MIND?

STOP IT! YOU'RE SCARING ME!

HEE HEE! I THINK IT'S CUTE!

GASP!

WHO IS THAT?

I'M **LUCINDA**, I JUST MOVED TO YOUR STREET. YOUR FRIEND IS **FUNNY**.

LOOSHKIN'S NOT FUNNY, **I'M** THE FUNNY ONE!

LOOK AT ME, I'M JUGGLING EGGS!

SPLOTCH! SPLOTCH! SPLOTCH!

THERE YOU ARE, LOOSHKIN. ARE YOU OKAY?

THBTHBTHH HHPTH

LOOSHKIN, WHAT ARE YOU DOING? DO YOU THINK YOU'RE FLYING A PLANE?

THPTBTHHH

*HONKK SCREEE THPTHBTHHHTHBTHHHH SCREEE

OHH NO.

YOU STAY OUT.

YOU'RE TRAMPLING ALL OVER MY PRIZED FLOWERS! THEY'RE MY EMOTIONAL SUBSTITUTE FOR A HAPPY CHILDHOOD!

STOMP! STOMP!

BOOHOOHOO! I'M SORRY I DROPPED ICE CREAM ON YOUR POSH TABLECLOTH, AUNTIE JEAN.

HEY, LOOSHKIN, WHAT'S GOING ON?

YOU'RE WORRYING A LOT OF PEOPLE.

WHAT ARE YOU DOING, LOOSHKIN?

GET AWAY! **GET AWAY!**

THPTHBTHH!

AW. ALL HE WANTED TO DO WAS BLOW A RASPBERRY IN BEAR'S FACE.

BLESS.

BLUGHH!

JAMIE

I DECLARE YOU TO BE AN ENEMY OF FROGTOPIA!

LOOSHKIN

THE CRAZ ADVENT OF...

WHAT IS DIS? SILLY CARTOONS?

THIS EPISODE:

I'M NOT TO BLAME.

WHAT A LOVELY DAY IT IS OUTSIDE! JUST THE RIGHT WEATHER TO STAY IN BED AND READ COMICS.

YOU SHOULD BE **OUTSIDE!** GARDENING!!

WHAT'S THIS? IS THIS A GAME?

JUST DO WHAT THE FROG SAYS.

AW, LOOSHKIN. YOU'RE PLAYING WITH A PUPPET?

THAT'S SWEET.

SINCE YOU WON'T COME OUT TO DO DA GARDENING, MISTER FROGBURT HAS BRINGED DE GARDENING TO YOU!!

SHRIEK!

CRASH!

I DID WARN YOU.

WE'RE NOT PLAYING. HE'S GONE MAD.

VERY FUNNY. NOW LEAVE ME ALONE.

LOOSHKIN

THE CRAZY ADVENTURES OF... ...THE MADDEST CAT IN THE WORLD!

THIS EPISODE: WOOO-OOOO-≋COUGH!≋ OOOO-OOOH!!

I STILL DON'T UNDERSTAND HOW ALL THESE BEES **GOT** INSIDE THE WASHING MACHINE.

I'VE A PRETTY GOOD IDEA.

ANYWAY, IT SHOULD BE FIXED NOW. LET'S TRY TURNING IT ON!

BOOP!

B-B-B-B-B-B!

UH OH.

RIDE IT LIKE A DONKEY!

YEEE HAW!

GASP! A FALSE WALL!

DOOSH!

DONK DONK DONK

SMASH!

RRGH! FINE! I SUPPOSE... WHERE'S HE GONE NOW?

SPIN SPIN!

HA HA! HA HA HA!

BARP! BARP! BARP! BARP!

ARMPIT FARTS? SERIOUSLY?

I HAVE A TIE, KEVIN!

I DON'T CARE ABOUT YOUR TIE.

PLAP!

EELS!

WHAT? WHY? WHY EELS?

WHY NOT EELS?

EELS MIGHT BE JUST WHAT WE NEED FOR OUR BIG NEW ADVERTISING CAMPAIGN!

HOW? WHAT? HOW?

FLIP! FLOP! FLIP! FLIP! FL—

EXPENSIVE TRAINERS

(GOT EELS IN THEM)

WELL, I THINK IT'S BRILLIANT!

EELS!

EVERYONE WILL WANT EELS IN THEIR SHOES.

EXPENSIVE TRAINERS

(GOT EELS IN THEM)

WELL DONE, MARCUS.

IT'S AN INSPIRED CAMPAIGN.

WHAT IS?

EXPENSIVE TRAINERS

I'M SO IMPRESSED, I'M MAKING YOU MANAGING DIRECTOR OF THE WHOLE COMPANY!

YOU'RE ME NOW. HERE ARE MY CAR KEYS.

THERE HE GOES, KEVIN. THE GREATEST CAT WHO EVER LIVED.

YOU'RE ALL CRAZY!

SCREE!

I HAVE A TIE, KEVIN!

BOOMP!

SCREE

LOOSHKIN'S BACK LATE TODAY.

PROBABLY BEEN ASLEEP UNDER A HEDGE.

LOOSHKIN

THE CRAZY ADVENTURES OF... ...THE MADDEST CAT IN THE WORLD!

THIS EPISODE:

NEE-NAW! NEE-NAW! NEE-NAW! NEE-NAW!

NEEEEENAWWW!

AHH- WHAT A BEAUTIFUL DAY! HOW LUCKY WE ARE TO...

NEEEEE YOWW! THPTBTH!

BUM CHEEKS!

A BEEEEE!

I'M SORRY, MRS JOHNSON, BUT YOUR HUSBAND'S INJURIES ARE VERY SERIOUS. THERE ARE VERY REAL CONSEQUENCES TO BEING SQUASHED BY A PLANE.

IN FACT, I WOULD ADVISE BED REST FOR THE NEXT THREE MONTHS.

OH NO, NOOOO!

BUT HOW WILL WE LOOK AFTER HIM? I HAVE TO WORK, AND MY TWO CHILDREN ARE IDIOTS!

THIS ISN'T A CARTOON, Y'KNOW.

NURSE LOOSHKIN WILL FIX HIM! RIGHT IN THE NUBBINS! BOSHING UP THE FLIPFLOPS! BRRURRP!

GNAW GNAW! YOUR TEMPERATURE IS SEVEN. I PRESCRIBE CHIPS.

CHIIIIIPS.

A-HEM!

OH FINE. WHAT'S THE WORST THAT CAN HAPPEN?

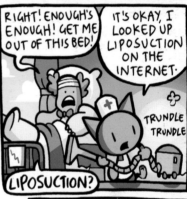

LOOSHKIN

THE CRAZY ADVENTURES OF... ...THE MADDEST CAT IN THE WORLD!

WHAT'S THE SMELLIEST THING IN THE WORLD?

SOCKS? NO!

DOG POOP! NO!

MOULDY CHEESE? NO!

IT'S MISTER ALAN FLOBBLESON, OF 152 THE DRIVE, YORKTON, KENT. HOI!

THIS EPISODE:

"WITH GREAT POWER COMES GIANT LASERS!"

PYEW!

BAH BAH BAH BAH BAH BAHHH BAH BAHBAH BAH BAH BUHH

MISTER PRESIDENT!

MISTER PRESIDENT!

MISTER PRESIDENT, THESE EXECUTIVE ORDERS YOU'RE ISSUING ARE MOST IRREGULAR!

THIS ONE'S JUST A DRAWING OF A SCREAMING HAT.

"INTERNATIONAL DANCE-OFFS"

"LETS BUILD DINOSAUR ISLAND"

"BROCCOLI TO BE ILLEGAL"

"SAUSAGE TUESDAYS"

SAUSAGES!

NO, NO NO!

YAYYY!

WHO SAID SAUSAGES? YOU KNOW THAT SETS HIM OFF.

SAUSAGES SAUSAGES ONK ONK ONKK!

MISTER PRESIDENT! MISTER PRESIDENT!

YOU HAVE TO MAKE SOME REAL POLICIES. ORDER SOMETHING FOR THE BENEFIT OF OUR COUNTRY!

HMM..

TAP TAP TAP!

?

SCREEEEAM!

SIR, THAT'S OUR MOST EXPENSIVE SPACE LASER! WE CAN'T JUST POINT IT AT TEDDY BEARS!

BUT HE'S SO ANNOYING!

LOOSHKIN

THE CRAZY ADVENTURES OF... ...THE MADDEST CAT IN THE WORLD!

ANNOUNCEMENT: DUE TO AN INCIDENT INVOLVING ANGRY CLOWNS, THERE NOW FOLLOWS A CHANGE IN OUR USUAL PROGRAMMING.

YOU KIDS BE CAREFUL KICKING THAT FOOTBALL ABOUT! I DON'T WANT IT HITTING MY PRIZE COLLECTION OF ANTIQUE WINEGLASSES.

OOF!! RIGHT IN THE PUDDINGS!

DOOSH!

"OOF! RIGHT IN THE PUDDINGS!" WILL CONTINUE AFTER THESE ADVERTS

OOF! RIGHT IN THE PUDDINGS!

OOF! OOF! RIGHT IN THE PUDDINGS! IN. THE. PUDDINGS!

LOOSHKIN, WHY DO YOU KEEP SAYING "OOF! RIGHT IN THE PUDDINGS"?

OOF! RIGHT IN THE PUDDINGS! GEARGH! PUNT!

UNF! OOF! RIGHT IN THE PUDDINGS!

RIGHT IN THE PUDDINGS! YOU WATCH IT TOO? THAT'S MY FAVOURITE SHOW!

WHAT SHOW?

THPTBTHHH

THPTBT

OOF! RIGHT IN THE PUDDINGS!

RIGHT IN THE PUDDINGS!

SPLOOSH!

IN THE PUDDINGS!

IN THE PUDDINGS!!

NEE NAW NEE NAW NEE

PUDDINGS, PUDDINGS! PUDDINGS! PUDDINGSSS!

SCREE

ROLL! ROLL! ROLL!

FWOOM!

HEE HEE HEE. OOF!

HEH HEH. RIGHT IN THE PUDDINGS!

WELCOME BACK TO PART TWO OF "OOF! RIGHT IN THE PUDDINGS!"

"OOF! RIGHT IN THE PUDDINGS!"

WHO ARE YOU TWO? AND WHY DO YOU SMELL LIKE PETROL?

SHH!

PUDDINGS.

ARGH! I FELL ON ME KIPPER!

A CHAIN OF EVENTS LATER...

ARGH! ME KIPPER!

I FELL ON ME KIPPER!

MAKE SOME
CLOWN NOISES!

EVERYONE I LOVE, I PUSH AWAY.

NO! FUNNY ONES! OH.

LOOSHKIN

THE CRAZY ADVENTURES OF...

...THE MADDEST CAT IN THE WORLD!

THIS EPISODE BEGINS WITH A DOORBELL

DING DONG!!

GET AWAYYYY!!

OH.

YOU'RE NOT THE CAT.

USUALLY HE'S WAITING FOR ME.

WATCHING.

POST

ANYWAY, I HAVE A PACKAGE FOR YOU.

MY OUTFITS!

To. Bear

OHH, THIS IS GOING TO BE SO MUCH FUN!

SLAM!

AND IT'S GOING TO CONFUSE THE HECK OUT OF LOOSHKIN.

zzzip!

BUKAWKKK! LOOK AT ME, LOOSHKIN! I'M A CHICKEN NOW!

OH FOR GOODNESS' SAKE!

YOU'RE A CHICKEN TOO?

WHAT DO YOU MEAN? I ALWAYS LOOK LIKE THIS.

FORGET IT!! I HAVE OTHER OUTFITS!

LOOK! I'M AN ELEPHANT NOW! BAROOO! ISN'T THAT WEIRD?

ISN'T WHAT WEIRD?

RRGH! RRGH!!

HOW ABOUT... A RABBIT?

NUP.

A FISH?

DING DONG!!

HOP HOP

IS HE GOING TO DROP SOMETHING ON ME?

IS THAT IT?

OCTOP...

NOPE.

NOT A PORK CHOP! OH, COME ON!

YEAH, YEAH, JUST GIVE ME THE PACKAGE.

IT'S A BIG ONE, I WARN YOU.

To: Bear

OH, BUT IT'LL BE WORTH IT...

...FOR NOW I AM BEARTRON!

WEARING A PERFECT REPLICA OF THE 1970s JAPANESE ANIME SUPERHERO SUIT.

EXQUISITELY CRAFTED AND SUPER RARE.

THERE'S NO WAY YOU'LL HAVE AN OUTFIT LIKE THIS!

WELL? WHAT DO YOU SAY, CAT?

THIS FIGHT IS OVER!

I HAVE WON WITH HONOUR! HA HA HA HA!

SPLASH!

YOU'VE SHORT-CIRCUITED IT. I'LL NEVER GET MY DEPOSIT BACK NOW!

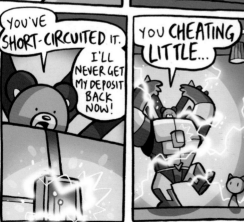

YOU CHEATING LITTLE...

BWO DOO OSH

ARGH!

I KNEW HE'D GET ME SOMEHOW!

CRUMP

LOOSHKIN

THE CRAZY ADVENTURES OF... ...THE MADDEST CAT IN THE WORLD!

Panel 1:
COME AND SEE WHAT I'VE DONE! **COME AND SEEEE!**

Panel 2:
LAST TIME YOU SAID THAT, MUM MADE ME HAND WASH ALL THE CURTAINS.

HEE! HEE! HEE! **HEE! HEE!!**

Panel 3:

I'VE HIDDEN BEAR UNDER THE CARPET!

YOU HAVE TO FIND HIM.

Panel 4:
OH WHAT FUNNN!

Panel 5:

LOOSHKIN! YOU CAN'T KEEP TREATING BEAR LIKE THIS!

Panel 6:

ALSO, HE'S THERE.

GAH! I MADE IT TOO EASY!

Panel 7:

HANG ON, I'LL PUSH THIS CUPBOARD OVER HIM...

SQU EE E ZE!

...THEN TRY AGAIN.

Panel 8:
WHAT'S HE DOING NOW?

BEAR! BEAR!

Panel 9:

BEAR?

Panel 10:

THEN WHO...

Panel 11:

SCREAMMM! SCREAM!

Panel 12:

RUN AWAY! IT'S GONE WRONG AGAIN!

WHAT A HAPPY HORSE!!

THANKS! I JUST REMEMBERED A FUNNY JOKE. NO ONE CARE!

LOOSHKIN

THE CRAZY ADVENTURES OF... ...THE MADDEST CAT IN THE WORLD!

FILMED IN FRONT OF A LIVE STUDIO AUDIENCE.

THAT'S YOUR FIFTH PULLED-PORK BUN!

WHAT CAN I SAY? I REALLY LIKE PULLED-PORK BUNS!

CHOMP CHOMP

HAHAHA!

BOILK!

UH OH. I REALLY NEED TO TOILET.

OOH! OOH! CLEAR A PATH!

I'M BUSTIN'!

THE TOILET

CHEER! HAHA!

HEY! WHO'S IN THERE? LET ME IN, I'M BUSTIN'!

TOILET

HAHA!

MASHED POTATO

CHEER! APPLAUSE!

RRRGHH! WHAT DO I DO? WHAT DO I DO? I HAVE TO GO SOMEWHERE!

I'M BUSTIN'!

NEXT DOOR...

HELLO? HELLO SANDRA? CAN I USE YOUR TOILET?

HAHAHA!

SORRY, SOMEONE'S ALREADY USING MINE.

WHAT? WHO?

APPLAUSE!

HAHA! AWWW!

198

199

NOT IN CINEMAS NOW

GRR!

ATTACK OF THE KILLER **TABLES!**

THE LAST THING YOU SEE...WILL BE A TABLE!

OK.

LOOSHKIN

THE CRAZY ADVENTURES OF...

...THE MADDEST CAT IN THE WORLD!

YAWWWNNNN!

WHAT A BEAUTIFUL DAY! I THINK I MIGHT...

20 POINTS!

SLAPPO!

~ROYAL~ PUMMMOO!

SHAKE SHAKE!

SHAKE-A SHAKE-A!

WHAT'S GOING ON? WHAT ARE YOU DOING?

WE ARE PLAYING **BIG CHOPS!** AND YOU ARE 20 POINTS DOWN!

THIS ISN'T FAIR! I DON'T KNOW HOW TO PLAY!

MINUS 10 POINTS!

RRGHHHHH! YOU'RE JUST MAKING THIS UP!

CHAIN SCORE!

SKOOSH!

+20 POINTS!

+30 POINTS!

FRRP! FRRP! FRRP! FRRP!

+50 POINTS!

HOP!

EEK!

BOING!

EUGH!

SKIDDDD

ON HIS BOTTOM!

A CHRISTMAS SPECIAL!!
LOOSHKIN

T'WAS THE NIGHT BEFORE CHRISTMAS, AND ALL THROUGH THE HOUSE.

HO! HO! HO! HO! HO! HO! HO! FRRP! PARP! SPLBPTH!

YOU'LL ALL BE GETTING THEM!

NOTHING WAS STIRRING, NOT EVEN A...

...MARZIPAN PIG?!

LOOOOOSHKIN! WAKE UP! I AM THE GHOST OF CHRISTMAS FUTURE!

YOU HAVE BEEN A VERY NAUGHTY CAT, SO THIS CHRISTMAS I HAVE DECIDED TO SHOW YOU THE ERROR OF YOUR WAYS.

DID YOU... DID YOU JUST EAT A BIT OF ME?

YOU WERE DELICIOUS!

FOR GOODNESS SAKE, DID YOU LISTEN TO A WORD I SAID?

SOMETHING ABOUT BUBBLE BATH?

YOU WILL BE VISITED BY THREE GHOSTS BEFORE CHRISTMAS MORN!

AND YOU'D BETTER LEARN SOMETHING, BUCKO!

HELLO.

I AM THE GHOST OF CHRISTMAS PAST! RIDE ME LIKE A PONY, AND WE WILL TRAVEL BACK INTO THE MISTS OF TIME!

ON IT!

PONY PONY PONY PONY!

WHAP! WHAP! WHAP!

BACK... BACK... BAAAAACK... MY BAAACK...

FLUMP

HERE WE ARE IN THE **OLDEN DAYS**, 1843! A BITTERLY COLD CHRISTMAS EVE, BEFORE POCKET HANDWARMERS WERE INVENTED.

YEUGH.

I KNOW, RIGHT?

LOOK, THERE IS YOUR GREAT-GREAT-GREAT-GREAT-GREAT-GREAT-GREAT-GRANDFATHER **JEBEDIAH LOOSHKIN**, STILL WORKING ON SUCH A NIGHT...

MISTER LOOSHKIN, SIR?

AH! BEAR SPROCKETTS, MY MOST LOYAL WORKER.

BUM

LOOK, I HAVE BEEN ETCHING A **BOTTOM**.

THAT'S VERY GOOD, SIR. I WAS WONDERING, SINCE IT'S CHRISTMAS EVE AND ME AND MY NINETEEN CHILDREN ARE STARVING, COULD WE HAVE A TINY SLITHER OF YOUR CHRISTMAS TURKEY?

TURKEY? WHAT TURKEY?

THE ONE BEHIND YOU.

OHHHH. **THAT** TURKEY.

NO. NO, YOU CAN'T. BECAUSE I'M A MEAN OLD CAT FROM THE OLDEN DAYS.

SO THRPBTHH!

WHAT A HEARTLESS THING TO DO, DON'T YOU AGREE?

JAM IT ON HIS HEAD!!

WHO...

WHAT A BRILLS IDEA!

HA HA HA! TURKEY HAT!

MMF! MMF! MMF!

TURKEY HAT BEAR!

HA HA!

I DON'T KNOW WHO YOU ARE, MYSTERIOUSLY HANDSOME CAT, BUT YOU'VE SHOWN ME THE **TRUE MEANING OF CHRISTMAS!**

JAMMING A TURKEY ONTO A BEAR'S HEAD!

WHAT? NO! THAT WASN'T THE POINT OF BRINGING YOU HERE!

HAVE SOME MONEY.

OKAY.

ALL OF YOU, SHUT IT!

BOSH!!

SANTA!

YAY, SANTA!

203

WHO MADE THESE HILARIOUS COMICS?

JAMIE SMART

has created colourful comics that have delighted children for over 20 years in the pages of publications such as *The Dandy*, *The Beano*, *The Phoenix*, and many more. He also creates children's books, including book for his ongoing multimedia project *Find Chaffy*.

JAMES TURNER

is a cartoonist, mathematician, and programmer from London, and his comic, *Star Cat*, won the Best Young People's Comic in the British Comic Awards. When not drawing comics, James enjoys board games, cooking, and making explosion noises with his mouth.

LAURA ELLEN ANDERSON

is a children's book author and illustrator who also crafts world-domination plans for Evil Emperor Penguin. When not working, Laura enjoys doodling, baking and making 'To Do' lists. Her trilogy of original novels, *Amelia Fang*, is being published by Egmont.

BY READING AND LAUGHING, YOU'VE HELPED HOLD THE UNIVERSE TOGETHER. THE COSMOS THANKS YOU. BUT, BEFORE WE PART, ALLOW ME TO INTRODUCE MY MANY LAB ASSISTANTS WHO PUT ALL THE COMICS TOGETHER!

GARY NORTHFIELD

is an award-winning author and illustrator. His bestselling *Julius Zebra* series is read worldwide. He lives with his dog, his twins and his partner Nicky. Together they have launched Bog Eyed Books, a showcase for UK comics.

JAMES STAYTE

is an illustrator and comic artist. He regularly works with the Royal National Lifeboat Institution, illustrating stories, posters, puzzles and more to help children learn how to stay safe near the water. He is exactly as muscular and as good at cooking as Gorebrah.

JESS BRADLEY

is an illustrator and designer of cute, colourful, and quirky characters. Her clients include *The Phoenix*, Capstone Publishing, Igloo Books, Genki Gear, UK Greetings, and Carlton Books. She enjoys drawing, video games, and drinking too much tea.